JOHNNY COME BACK

Eighty-Four Days of Miracles

Claudia Randolph

with Madelyn Rohrer

This book is dedicated to:

All of the doctors, nurses, therapists, and other medical and hospital personnel who were involved with Johnny's care.

Members of both our families who put us foremost in their lives and were with us physically, spiritually and emotionally.

Pastor Karen Lane of Jonesborough United Methodist Church, the Sisters of Faith group, and other church members who supported us through our ordeal.

...And especially to my husband, Johnny.

Johnny Randolph before his 2017 illness

Thank you to my contributors and proofreaders:
Victoria Ingalls
Carole Marks
Henrietta Paulsen
Jerry Paulsen
Madelyn Rohrer
Jane Townsend

Introduction

Faith is a personal experience, not seen, but felt and embraced. I never knew how much faith I had until this unexpected event happened to Johnny and me.

I have been "a believer" since childhood, but not always living as I should. I would be in and out of church throughout my entire life, but yet always believing. For the past fifteen years, my faith in God has really grown, but I never knew how much faith *I really had* until I was tested time and time again... until I went through eighty-four days with my husband, Johnny, who was in the hospital in critical, often life-and-death situations. That was when I found out how deep my faith really was. It was an awakening for me.

One of the things I learned on this journey was that God always put someone in our path who needed to be there and at precisely the right time. That alone created many miracles within our story. It has been a testimony of God's *continuous* presence.

It was also not too long into this journey that I realized my <u>real</u> hope for Johnny's recovery did not come from physicians but through my faith in God and what God had control over. There were many times when Johnny was on the proverbial doorstep of death; when family was called in; when he was totally dependent on life-sustaining machines; when I was given little hope by physicians for his survival. Yet *something* deep inside of him rallied each time and he managed to pull through.

While I am thankful for and have the utmost respect for what the physicians and medical personnel continually did to keep Johnny alive, I have also learned to appreciate the significance of *praying without ceasing*. I prayed silently alone as well as with Johnny so he could hear...and he did. Even in his darkest moments, he heard my voice; he knew I was there. It kept him in touch with the physical world *and* the spiritual world *and* the connection between the two. I especially want to share that piece of information with my readers. If you have ever wondered if someone can hear and understand voices and be able to process what they are hearing while physically unable to communicate or respond, the answer is definitely yes! What you say and how you say it are important!

Another reason I am writing this book is to stress the importance of having an advocate who knows you well and is willing and able to be with you in an adverse medical situation...someone who knows or has access to your medical history, or at least enough of it so that he/she can assist your doctors by contributing pertinent information if you are unable to do so yourself. Whether you are a patient or an advocate, it is important to think ahead and be prepared for any medical emergency.

I hope that by walking our walk through the pages of this book, our experience will be of help to others who may find themselves on a similar journey, especially those who may at times feel abandoned, confused, or be facing what seems to be a hopeless situation.

This is my own personal testimony as a nurse, wife, and advocate/caregiver of what healing, hope, and faith really mean, both medically and spiritually. Never give up hope. Never stop praying. Never stop believing. You are not alone.

Claudia Randolph

Notes from the Writer

As an author and oral storyteller, I often have an opportunity to be a listener as well as a teller. I consider it a privilege when someone is led to tell me one of their own stories. Most of the time it is humorous, either family or work-related, but sometimes it is about a more serious experience – emotional, spiritual, or even hard-to-explain. Whatever the genre, however, the true treasure is spending quality time listening and learning with those who are willing to share their story.

But every once in a while…I hear a story that makes its way into my heart and doesn't leave – one that seasoned storytellers refer to as "needing to be told." I heard that expression for the first time many years ago in a storytelling workshop when the facilitator said: "If a story *wants* to be told, or *needs* to be told, it will find someone to tell it." While it didn't mean much to me then, I have learned to appreciate the strange truth in that tenet. That's the way it was with Claudia Randolph's story when she told it on May 10, 2018.

It was at the monthly meeting of the Sisters of Faith from the United Methodist Church in Jonesborough, Tennessee, and it was the first time Claudia had been with the group since November 2017. "Sisters of Faith" is an organization of about three dozen very busy can-do women who purposely take the time to pull away from their families and careers once a month to enjoy a relaxed evening of fun and business. It consists of dinner, preferably in someone's home rather than in a noisy restaurant, a short and to-the-point business discussion, and a devotional.

By chance, I happened to be sitting directly across the dinner table that evening from Claudia, unaware that she was going to be doing the devotional. It was a recap of the horrendous ordeal that she and her husband had been through for months. I looked directly into her face and her eyes as she related the story that personally resonated with all of us. Why was it so personal for Sisters of Faith? Because we had walked the journey with her, medically and spiritually, through almost daily text messages – the easiest way for her to communicate from hospitals, medical buildings, and rehab facilities.

Her devotional was, of necessity, short – just twenty minutes. While it barely scratched the surface of what she had been through, it came directly from her heart. It spoke of something much deeper than her medical expertise. It also spoke of humanness – sometimes over and above what one could expect, and other times human failure. And then there was her faith...true, trusting, and steadfast faith.

After that very profound, emotional twenty minutes, I knew I had come face to face with one of those incredible stories that wanted/needed to be told.

I am honored that Claudia and Johnny have allowed me to help them tell their story.

Madelyn Rohrer

Please note that a Glossary of Medical Terms is included at the back of this book for reference.

Table of Contents

Christmas 2017

Claudia Randolph would have no way of knowing when she took her husband Johnny to the Emergency Room on the night of December 22, 2017 to be treated for the flu that they would not return home for eighty-four days. They would be whisked out of town with no time for preparation, no time to think about anything...other than saving Johnny's life.

December has always been a special month for the Randolph family. In addition to the Christian observance of Christmas as the birth of the Christ Child and all of the festivities of the season, Johnny celebrated his 66th birthday on December 13, and Claudia celebrated her 63rd birthday on December 19. Sometimes birthdays and "the holidays" blended together, depending on who could be around to help celebrate. This year, the out-of-towners Sasha and Chris, Claudia's daughter and son-in-law, were expected to arrive a couple days before Christmas so they could spend some relaxing, quality family time together. The tree was up and decorated, as was the rest of their stately historic home in downtown Jonesborough, Tennessee. Most of the shopping was done and colorfully-wrapped presents were under the tree. Christmas 2017 would certainly be one to remember, but not for the usual reasons.

JOHNNY COME BACK

<u>Thursday, December 21, 2017</u>

It started on December 21st – a busy day, but nothing out of the norm. Claudia and her mother, Gerry, were at Vanderbilt Hospital in Nashville for Gerry's regularly-scheduled visit with a neurologist. They had left their home in Jonesborough the day before and spent the night close to the hospital. The 270-mile trip was long for Claudia's 89-year-old mother, so they always did it in two days – one day over, stay overnight, early morning appointment and return home the next day.

Early in the morning, Claudia tried calling Johnny as she always did to start the day, but there was no answer. It was unusual for him to not answer his phone. Johnny and Claudia have always talked several times a day whenever they were apart.

When he called back later in the morning, he sounded terrible. "I've been to Urgent Care, Claudia. Felt terrible this morning – dizzy, weak, light-headed, disoriented. They told me I've got the flu and gave me a prescription. I got it filled and now I'm in bed, just lying here and resting. Take your time and be careful coming home. I love you."

While he didn't go into detail right then about *how* weak he was, Claudia later learned that a friend of theirs also happened to be at Urgent Care when Johnny walked in. As soon as she realized how sick he was, she was instantly at his side, holding him up by his britches so he wouldn't fall over. She stayed near him, offering to help him to the exam room when it was his turn, but he refused.

Diagnosed as having the flu, Johnny left the clinic with a prescription for Tamiflu® and headed to his pharmacy. They were closed – it was too early to be opened for business yet. He could have waited, but he felt too miserable. He just wanted to go home, take some medicine, and go to bed. He went to another pharmacy but, by this time, he was so weak he couldn't walk in the door. Instead, he drove up to the window. Realizing that he was very sick, pharmacy personnel obligingly rushed out to the car to help him and take his information. He vaguely remembered driving home and getting into the house. From this point forward, he would remember very little.

***

On their way back to Jonesborough that afternoon, Claudia called Sasha and Chris who were getting packed and ready to head out from their home in Newport Richey, Florida. "Johnny's got the flu, Sasha. You might not want to come."

"Oh, no. I'm so sorry to hear that, Mom, but we'll be careful. We won't get near Johnny until he feels better and is not contagious anymore. We really want to be there for Christmas."

"From the way he sounded, he's probably going to spend most of his time in the bedroom anyway," Claudia assured her. "See you tomorrow."

Claudia and Gerry got home around 7:00 p.m. and the first thing Claudia wanted to do after she got her mom settled was check on Johnny. His face was warm, not unusual with the flu. He didn't want anything to eat, just drink. She got the car unloaded, went back out to the store, and bought anything she thought he might want to drink. Still believing that Johnny had the flu, she decided to sleep on the couch - close enough to hear him, but far enough away

3

that he wouldn't be breathing on her. Nothing out of the ordinary occurred that night other than just being in a "sick house."

<u>Friday, December 22</u>

December 22nd did not start out particularly well. Claudia's phone died early in the day...completely. She had been having problems with it for a while but just hadn't taken the time to figure it out. Now she had no choice – it was dead! But she wasn't surprised. She always said in a joking way, "If it's going to happen, it's going to happen to me!" That was the first thought that went through her head, but it wasn't funny right now – it was frustrating!

Why now? she asked herself almost angrily. *I've got things to do. Johnny is sick. The kids are coming in. It's almost Christmas. Why does this have to happen <u>now</u>? Because if it is going to happen, it is going to happen to me, and not necessarily at a convenient time,* she reminded herself. *That's why!*

It turned out to be a perfect example of the proverbial "blessing in disguise." It did not take her long to realize that it could not have happened at a *better* time. It would be her main contact with the outside world for the next eighty-four days.

When she got home in the middle of the afternoon, Johnny was still in bed. She decided to let him sleep. Being a nurse, she knew that rest was more important than food for someone with the flu. Dinner wasn't anything special that night, just something quick for her mother and herself and for Sasha and Chris when they arrived. She looked in on Johnny again around 10:00 pm; even if he didn't want to eat, she had to get some fluids into him.

To her horror, his condition had changed drastically from the last time she looked in on him. He was shaking so bad the bed was actually moving and he was sweating profusely. She took his temperature. It was 104.2. There was no hesitation – he had obviously taken a turn for the worse and needed to be in the hospital. He was weak but able to walk. She got him into the car and made the twenty-minute drive to Johnson City. It was late and it was a Friday night. As a former Emergency Room nurse, she knew that the Emergency Room would most likely be packed. She made the decision to go to Franklin Woods Hospital, a smaller hospital a short distance from the much larger Johnson City Medical Center. Being a smaller hospital, she reasoned, it might not be as busy. Johnny could be treated quicker and they could get back home sooner.

It turned out to be not a good decision. Johnny was much sicker than previously thought. This was more than the flu...much more! It was the beginning of a nightmare.

***

Treatment started immediately. Johnny was in septic shock (a widespread infection that can cause organ failure and dangerously low blood pressure – a toxic condition). They gave him three liters of fluid. At first, they thought he might have had a heart attack, but the EKG was normal. However, his troponin (a marker indicating damage to the heart muscle – done with a blood draw) was elevated. The normal range is 0.0 to 0.4. Johnny's was 1.9! They managed to get one IV line in, but couldn't get another one in – his veins had constricted from dehydration and sepsis.

His condition was critical. The decision was made to transfer him to the Johnson City Medical Center (JCMC) – there was no other choice.

Saturday, December 23

Shortly after midnight on December 23, while arrangements for a transfer were being made, the Franklin Woods staff physician suggested that family should be called in. Claudia was stunned and almost numb as she made the calls. Sasha and Chris had already arrived at the Randolph home and were able to get to Franklin Woods Hospital by 1:30 a.m., just before Johnny was transferred to the Johnson City Medical Center.

Johnny's son and daughter, Joshua and Jennifer, went directly to the Med Center. Joshua was working at the East Tennessee State University Security Department in Johnson City and came straight from work, arriving at 3:00 a.m. Jennifer was so upset she couldn't drive. Her stepfather drove her to the hospital from her home in the neighboring town of Erwin, about a fifteen-mile distance. She arrived about the same time as her brother.

***

Sasha and Chris waited at Franklin Woods with Claudia until Johnny was ready for transfer, then went back to the house. They didn't want to leave "Grandmom" (Gerry) alone any longer. She had been asleep when they received the call from Claudia and they didn't want to wake her, knowing she would worry. She still didn't know they had left. Claudia followed the ambulance alone in her car.

The hospital *was* very busy, just as Claudia anticipated. Although he was critically ill, Johnny was placed in a step-down room upon arrival at the JCMC rather than ICU. When Claudia got to Johnny's room, the nurses were trying to get an IV in him as they awaited orders from the accepting physician. They were not being successful. The nurses didn't know what had transpired up to this time, but Claudia did. She was the <u>only one</u> who knew the severity of Johnny's condition right then – and she was getting annoyed and frustrated by what she saw was happening and what she knew *should be happening but wasn't.* With Johnny's two children standing in the corner of his room with shock and concern on their faces, not knowing what was going on or understanding the seriousness of the situation themselves, Claudia's nursing experience, instinct, and adrenalin kicked in! It had to – she knew Johnny was crashing!

"I want to see the house supervisor and I want to see her now!" she snapped. The surprised nurses cautiously explained that there is a process that must be done. "I know there is a process, but there is also a protocol," she insisted. "He should have had his troponin redrawn and it should have been done before now. He should have another IV in...and I want to see the house supervisor!"

Soon she heard a little sweet voice coming around the corner – a very distinctive *but familiar* voice. Claudia turned around and found herself looking into the face of her long-time friend, Joy – someone she started nursing school with in 1982, someone she had seen only occasionally over the past 35 years!

"Joy!" Claudia exclaimed with frustration and relief!

"Claudia!" was the response. They quickly hugged and then Joy got down to business!

7

Everything turned around right then. Joy tried to get an IV in Johnny herself but couldn't. The next thing Claudia knew, they were wheeling him out of the step-down room heading for Cardiac ICU. When they got there, cardiologists and intensivists were waiting. Johnny's blood pressure was dropping: 56/34; his heart rate was increasing: 136; his respirations were increasing: 30-34; and he was still sweating profusely. He was very close to death – but Joy's presence and interceding made the difference with Johnny getting the attention he needed. Claudia, Joshua, and Jennifer kept watch and waited for the results of tests.

At some point that night, a nurse anesthetist who was also a personal friend from church, walked into Johnny's room. Claudia hardly recognized him dressed in his scrubs (operating room attire) rather than his street clothes. "I was walking through ICU and saw you sitting here," he said. "What's going on with Johnny?" He could only stay for a few minutes, but the sight of another familiar face and presence of a friend meant a lot at a time when support and comfort were needed.

After numerous tests, Johnny was diagnosed with myocarditis, inflammation of the heart muscle. His blood pressure pretty much stabilized during the night, leading the doctors to the decision that it would be safe to transfer him back to a cardiac step-down unit the next day. His myocarditis seemed related to, or at least possibly relevant to, a new medicine he was taking for a previous condition: Myasthenia Gravis, an autoimmune disease.

***

Johnny's history of Myasthenia Gravis, explained by Claudia:

"Johnny was first diagnosed with Myasthenia Gravis in 2015, over two and a half years ago. He had been complaining for months about not being able to see, blaming it on his glasses. I kept telling him to go get his eyes checked. Finally, he did, and was told there really wasn't that much change in his eyesight. But he was still having trouble seeing. On that same day, while driving home from the optometrist's office, he said his right eyelid 'fell' and he couldn't open it. Because he is legally blind in his left eye, he could now no longer see to drive. He did the only thing he could think of at that time – he took his left hand and lifted his eyelid up so he could see to drive home. He held it up all the way home.

"We immediately made a doctor appointment which was a couple of days later but, during the interim, Johnny taped his eyelid up during the day with electrical tape. Being a nurse, of course, I did my homework and researched Johnny's condition before our appointment day arrived so I had a pretty good idea of was going on. There were strong indications of Myasthenia Gravis – an autoimmune disease that produces weakness and rapid fatigue of muscles under voluntary control. When I asked the physician about that possibility, however, he did not agree. He said Johnny's condition was neurological and would require a Neurology consult.

"That's when I didn't agree! I felt he should have an ophthalmology consult as well as a neurological consult but the physician said he would refer us only to a neurologist. He did not feel that ophthalmology would be able to treat whatever was going on. The appointment we received with the neurologist was months away.

"As we went out to the car, my mind started processing all that had transpired and I felt it just wasn't right – plus I didn't feel particularly good about Johnny having to walk around for months with his eyelid taped up. I called another friend from church who

9

works with ophthalmologists in Johnson City, and explained what was going on. Her first comment was, 'I'll bet he has Myasthenia Gravis.' That was 11:15 in the morning. 'Can you be here by noon?' she asked.

"I'll be anywhere you want me to be, I told her. We were there by noon and Johnny was seen by an ophthalmologist – one of the very few in our area who deal with this condition. Titers were drawn (blood levels that indicate certain antibodies in the system), and all the labs came back with high levels. Myasthenia Gravis was confirmed. Johnny became his patient and was put on medications to help with the symptoms of weakness and eye droop. I became his caregiver and designated driver for two months until the medications kicked in. I will always be thankful to our special friend who helped us get the correct diagnosis and treatment.

"We still kept the appointment with the neurologist. Between him and the ophthalmologist, Johnny's Myasthenia Gravis has been kept under control."

***

So, what exactly is Myasthenia Gravis and why did the doctors attach it to Johnny's condition on December 23rd?

"It is an autoimmune disease that attacks the muscles and weakens the immune system," Claudia explains. "If a person has a weakened immune system, as Johnny does, it unfortunately carries with it an additional cause for concern: Cytomegalovirus (CMV). CMV is a common virus that can infect almost anyone. Once infected, your body retains the virus for life. Most people don't even know they have CMV because it rarely causes problems in healthy people. When the doctors at the Johnson City Medical Center learned about Johnny's Myasthenia Gravis condition, they automatically tested him for CMV.

The test came back negative so they ruled it out as a contributing factor and continued to look for another cause of the myocarditis."

The doctors and Claudia were juggling multiple issues. Considering the blood pressure stabilization and elimination of the possibility of CMV, there was a third factor that entered into the decision to transfer Johnny back to the cardiac step-down unit. Johnny's medications had been changed the first week in December. He had been feeling weak and short of breath and his neurologist felt he would benefit from a different medication for his Myasthenia Gravis. He was placed on Azathioprine®, the generic name for Imuran®, a drug used to suppress the immune system. Imuran is commonly used to treat patients who have undergone kidney transplantation and for diseases in which modifying the activity of the immune system is important. It is a type of chemo drug.

Going with the best information they had at the time, the doctors decided that Johnny did not need to be kept in Cardiac ICU. He could safely be moved to a Cardiac step-down unit while they continued to look for the cause of his heart condition.

However – if Johnny's test for CMV would have come back positive, his treatment would possibly have moved in a different direction, to a much different level...but even though it came back negative, CMV was <u>not</u> out of the picture!

Sunday, December 24

Christmas Eve morning seemed to be the turning point for Johnny. His blood pressure was continuing to stabilize and his heart rate had improved through the night. Arrangements were being made to move him to a Cardiac step-down unit some time that day. By early afternoon, Claudia felt it was safe to leave his side for a late lunch/dinner combination in the hospital cafeteria. On the way back, she ran into her friend, Joy, the nursing supervisor.

"Johnny is on the schedule to be moved to a step-down unit, Claudia, but there's no bed available. With this being the flu season, the hospital is packed, as I'm sure you can appreciate. If you don't mind, even if a room does become available, I want to leave him in ICU for another day. I just have a feeling he shouldn't be moved yet."

That was fine with Claudia. The important thing was that he was getting better. But Joy's "feeling" about leaving him in ICU for another day turned out to be almost a premonition. When Claudia got back to the room about 4:00 p.m., Johnny had again taken a turn for the worse. His blood pressure had dropped critically low; his heart rate and respirations were up. He was struggling to breathe. She ran out and got his nurse, who looked at the monitor next to the bed and responded: "His MAP is fine." (MAP is mean arterial pressure. It is the average blood pressure in an individual during a single cardiac cycle).

But Claudia's patience was not fine! Her nursing experience kicked in once again. "It was fine yesterday, too, when he was crashing! Look at him! Treat the patient, not the monitor!"

The nurse hurried out, leaving Claudia to watch Johnny, who was steadily deteriorating. She waited...and waited, for what seemed like an eternity. Finally, with frustration at a peak, she went out and asked to see an intensivist and the cardiologist. The nurse explained that they had already signed Johnny off to his family physician, who had been called three times and had not called back yet. There was nothing else he could do except wait.

Claudia didn't care about protocol right then! "So what are you going to do, let him die?" she asked angrily. But she had to resign herself to the fact that there was no one around who could help. She went back into the room, held Johnny's hand, and continued to watch the monitor while she waited for *"someone" to call or come in...or "something" to be done!*

It was around 8:00 p.m. when two night-shift supervisors came to the entrance of the room. "Joy called from home and asked us to come and check on you," one of them said. "Is there anything you need? Is there anything we can do for you?"

"Yes!" Claudia exploded. "Yes! "I want a cardiologist in here! I want an intensivist in here! I want Infectious Disease in here! I want *something* done."

They looked at Johnny, saw his worsening condition and Claudia's concern, and hurried back out. Almost immediately, there was an intensivist and cardiologist in the room. Infectious Disease would not be available until morning, she was told. The resident cardiologist and intensivist reassessed Johnny and saw there had been a drastic change since he had been discharged to go to the step-down unit. Claudia silently thanked Joy for "her feeling" and that Johnny had not been transferred out of ICU as planned.

There were now multiple people working with him, and Claudia knew they were doing everything they could. She stood at the desk just outside the door to Johnny's room while the intensivist talked on the phone with the cardiac surgeon. She heard the cardiac surgeon responding that he would do whatever was needed.

"We don't have time for consent forms," the intensivist said as he walked back in and proceeded to insert an arterial line in Johnny's wrist (measures the blood pressure through the arteries) and a Swan-Ganz™ catheter (a thin tube or catheter inserted into the right side of the heart and the arteries leading to the lungs. It is done to monitor the heart's function and blood flow and pressures in and around the heart. This test is most often done in people who are critically ill.).

Johnny was sweating profusely and continuing to deteriorate but was still alert. He kept asking for ice water with Sweet 'N Low® although no one really knew why he wanted the Sweet 'N Low. His legs were beginning to mottle; his hands were grey and numb – signs that the body was trying to keep blood in vital organs to preserve them. His body was shutting down.

He went into cardiogenic shock, a condition in which the heart suddenly can't pump enough blood to meet the body's needs. It is often fatal if not treated immediately; only half of the people with this condition survive. His liver and kidneys had already begun to shut down. The cardiologist was there and talked to Claudia about taking him into surgery to insert an impella – a device inserted through the groin into an artery and threaded up to the heart to temporarily assist in moving blood through the heart and the rest of the organs in the body. This was something new to Claudia. Her nursing career had been in the Emergency Room, not ICU or operating rooms. She agreed to the procedure.

Johnny was taken into surgery and the procedure completed. Afterward, he was moved to a larger room in ICU for more ease of multiple people working with him at one time. It was now 11:00 p.m. Christmas Eve. Although he was "holding his own" after surgery, he was still critical with dwindling chances for survival. "Vanderbilt" was being mentioned.

Monday, December 25 – Christmas Day

Claudia's new phone was now her constant companion. She reached out for spiritual support from her Sisters of Faith with a text message to Pam, the SOF leader:

"Please find it in your heart to pray for my husband, Johnny. He is in ICU and has been diagnosed with viral myocarditis."

A flurry of text messages and phone calls followed as the text was forwarded to the group's members.

Follow-up text from Claudia: "He has not done well. Both chambers of his heart have just about quit pumping. They put in an impella to rest the heart. If this doesn't work, they will airlift to Vanderbilt. Should know maybe around 10 or so this am. Pray!"

Pam sent out another message: "Johnny's not doing well at all folks. Claudia says they may need to airlift him to Vanderbilt later this morning. Pray HARD for him this Christmas morning!"

The request for prayers spread rapidly in Tennessee and throughout the country wherever people were traveling for the holidays. As time went on, more and more people were added to the special group of texters praying for Johnny...friends, strangers, and family. These people became her lifeline to the outside world.

Around 11:00 a.m. Claudia decided to lift the sheet to rub Johnny's feet and saw in horror that the foot on the leg the impella had been placed in was turning black and the leg was mottled. The vein in his leg had occluded (blocked off) and the blood was not able to be pumped back to his heart. The foot and leg were dying. The additional concern now was how to save his leg as well as his heart.

Vascular was called in for an assessment of what could be done to save the leg. Amputation of the leg was recommended, but they said it could not be done until the heart was stable enough for surgery. In his present condition, he would most likely not pull through. They left the decision up to Cardiology. Without that decision, there was nothing more they could do...and they left.

It was now a "life or limb" situation: leg or heart. If the impella were pulled to save the leg, the heart would still not be able to pump enough blood to sustain his body. The heart would die. Because the impella was in the groin, Vascular felt that by pulling it out, Johnny would be vulnerable to the additional complication of infection if anything invasive needed to be done.

Meanwhile, Johnny was having increasing trouble breathing and was intubated (a procedure whereby a tube is placed down the throat and breathes oxygen into the lungs for the patient and is regulated by a ventilator). Johnny had refused the ventilator at first because his practical side said "it costs too much." Claudia assured him the finances would all work out and explained it would not be forever; it would help him breathe and he could rest better. Trying to breathe was wearing him out, however, and he finally conceded, but with the added stipulation of "no more than two to three weeks at the most!" He was sedated for the procedure and was kept sedated.

His condition was critical. Airlifting to Vanderbilt Hospital was mentioned again but there was mounting concern that he would not survive the flight, regardless of what decisions were made.

To Johnny's family, it was like walking through a bad dream as they struggled to understand how he got from the wrong diagnosis of "having the flu" three days ago to the very real probability of imminent death – at the Johnson City Medical Center, en route to Vanderbilt Hospital in Nashville, or perhaps after arriving at Vanderbilt. It just didn't seem possible.

But at this moment, there was not much choice – it was still a life or limb decision. The cardiologist emphasized that Johnny could live without his leg, but he couldn't live without a heart, but there was no real solution offered from either Vascular or Cardiology.

"So, you're telling me that Johnny is going to die here or he is going to die at Vanderbilt?" a distraught Claudia asked.

"He will probably die on the way" the cardiologist said bluntly. Then he excused himself for a few minutes and left the room while Claudia, Joshua, and Jennifer absorbed the dire outlook.

Visions started running through Claudia's head like clips of a futuristic movie. She saw her husband in a wheel chair, on crutches, learning how to walk with one leg. She pictured him trying to work in his garden, riding his tractor. At the age of 66, this would be a real adjustment and lifestyle change. It would be hard for him. And what about his heart? They still didn't know what was going on with his heart!

"I want to go to Vanderbilt," Claudia decided when the cardiologist returned.

"I think that would be a good idea," he agreed, and proceeded to make the arrangements.

It was not that easy, however, and Claudia knew it. She had spent time working in the Call Center where arrangements like this were made. It was always a busy place, taking calls from all over the region. It was where arrangements for transfers between hospitals were made; where doctors and nurses conferenced between hospitals. Wings Air Rescue also resided within those four walls.

Claudia thought back to all the times she had worked with Joy on getting beds for patients who needed to be transferred. Working in the ER, she made those arrangements herself many times. She had worked both ends of the spectrum...helping to load outgoing patients into the helicopters and riding in the ambulance with incoming patients. It was unimaginable to realize that she was now doing this for her own husband!

Consequently, she knew that before a transfer could take place, everything had to be in order. There had to be a receiving physician, a bed available, a helicopter available, and good flying weather.

"It may not happen until tomorrow," she was told.

Then there were more chilling words from the cardiologist as he stood over Johnny: "He has taken a turn for the worse." There was nothing more he could do. "I am going home," he said, and left the room – just as Vascular had done.

Feelings of doom, frustration and disappointment swept over Claudia. *IT IS Christmas Day,* she acknowledged – *a day for family.* But she still couldn't accept it. She felt abandoned by the medical personnel, standing alone on Christmas Day with her husband's life hanging in the balance. She thought back on her career as an Emergency Room nurse and all the hands she held as people passed away and all the families she comforted and cried with. It never made any difference what day it was. *No, this is not the way it's supposed to be at the end of someone's life!* she thought angrily. *Thank God for the nurses who are continuing to do everything possible to keep Johnny alive!* She became convinced more than ever that they *had to get to Vanderbilt...somehow, and quickly.*

She looked down at her phone and the plethora of text messages from all of her prayer warriors and sent out another text explaining what was going on. They immediately started texting back and it heartened her to know that friends were listening and responding. She stood over Johnny, reading each text. Even though he was sedated and intubated, she knew he could hear and understand even if he couldn't respond. Then a very precious text came through from a family friend and hospice nurse, Jan Magee – a text they would always remember: "May this be Johnny's Christmas Miracle."

A Christmas miracle! Yes, that is what we need, she thought silently. *Please, God, send us a miracle!*

19

At that very moment, the miracle happened, or at least it seemed like it did. A nurse appeared at the door and said, "Vanderbilt is on their way!"

But even as Claudia was clinging to a thread of renewed hope, Johnny's condition was continuing to worsen. She knew they were racing against the clock. The possibility he wouldn't even make it to Vanderbilt was looming above them like a dark cloud. Her heart sank when she heard later that Vanderbilt was <u>not</u> on the way after all. She wasn't told why. Maybe something *was not* in place. Maybe it was felt that Johnny should not be moved for some reason. She felt numb – like being alone even though there were people around. It was like standing in a void, not knowing or having any control over what was happening.

Suddenly, and for no obvious reason, she felt uplifted – washed with a new and strange feeling, something she had not felt since the nightmare started – **peace!** It was settling over her like a gentle blanket. *Suddenly,* she knew she was not alone after all. Was God sending them a miracle? Or was he giving them peace to face an inevitable outcome?

She thought about Joy. *Should I bother her at home on Christmas Day? Yes,* she decided; *Joy would want to know what is going on - plus I really just want to talk to her – to hear her voice.*

Joy's response was, "I'll be right there!"

While she waited for Joy, the miracle took place. Dr. Charles Raudat, a Cardio-Thoracic surgeon she had not yet met was walking through ICU when a nurse stopped him and asked him to look at Johnny's chart. He did. Then he laid the chart down, walked into Johnny's room and, without introducing himself, pulled the sheet up on his bed, exposing the foot and leg. He saw for himself the foot that was now black, the leg that was mottled and worsening, and said, "I can fix this." He walked back to the door, stopped and turned around, and said to Claudia and her family, "We will be in surgery in 30 minutes."

"Who was that?" a surprised Jennifer asked Claudia.

"I don't know."

While Johnny was being prepared for surgery, Dr. Raudat went out to the nurses' station, personally called Vanderbilt, and made all the necessary arrangements.

When Joy arrived around 2:00 in the afternoon, her presence was like a breath of fresh air. She proceeded to find out details from the nurses and kept Claudia informed. There was not much time for talking; things were happening quickly – Johnny's life was slipping away. "They are going to remove the impella and do a fasciotomy," Joy told her as Johnny was being wheeled into surgery. (Fasciotomy is a procedure consisting of three incisions placed vertically in the lower leg to relieve pressure and help save the leg.) "Then he is going to be placed on ECMO support. It is his only chance."

"What is ECMO?" Claudia asked.

Joy tried to explain it: extracorporeal membrane oxygenation – a temporary mechanical support system used to aid heart and lung function on patients with severe respiratory and/or cardiac failure. She Googled® it on her phone and let Claudia read it. As

Johnny was undergoing surgery, Claudia was reading on line what was happening to him.

They waited. Even with the impella removed, a fasciotomy performed, and ECMO, Johnny's chances for survival remained tenuous at best. His body was weak; his heart was weak; they could still lose him. Her mind was racing with visions of what life would be like without Johnny. She tried to calm her mind with reasoning: *It would certainly be different, yes, but I've been alone before. I've faced a lot of challenges in my life; I'm a survivor. Yeah, I'd be okay...but that's not what I want! I love my life with Johnny. I want to continue our life together. I want another Valentine's Day. I want another wedding anniversary. I want another Christmas together. This is not the way any Christmas should end!* She kept trying to focus on her trust in medical procedures as well as her faith in God, which had now become more important than at any time in her life, but the dreaded scenario kept pushing its way into her mind. She shared her painful thinking with Joy. "What am I going to do next Christmas?"

Joy's response was instantaneous: "You are going to look back and say this was a Christmas miracle!"

It was the second time she heard that term in a matter of hours. Jan's wish of "May this be Johnny's Christmas Miracle" immediately came back into her mind. It was what she needed to hear.

A nurse came by and announced, "Vanderbilt is on the way," and this time they really were...but with a plane, not a helicopter.

Joy remained until the surgery was almost over; then left to go to her daughter's home for Christmas dinner, reminding Claudia that she would continue to be just a phone call away.

At the Randolph house, Sasha and Chris cooked Christmas dinner for Gerry, with the intent of providing some semblance of Christmas for her and to try to keep her from worrying. Then Gerry stayed home while Sasha and Chris brought Christmas dinner to Claudia, Jennifer and Joshua in the ICU waiting area: turkey, cranberry sauce, roasted vegetables and pumpkin and cherry pie. The smell of food reminded Claudia that she had not eaten since the day before and was famished. Food and rest were two luxuries that had eluded her. As she ate her Christmas dinner in the waiting room, she wondered where her next meal would be – Johnson City? Nashville? She didn't know and it really didn't matter. All she knew for sure was that while they were sitting around a table in ICU waiting, Johnny was in surgery fighting for his life.

The timing was perfect! As the last suture was being placed, the physician from Vanderbilt was knocking on the Operating Room door, ready to pick Johnny up. Dr. Raudat came out, shook Claudia's hand...that hand that had just saved her husband's leg, heart, and life...and said "Merry Christmas."

***

In Johnny's condition, he could not have been transported in a helicopter as Claudia first assumed – it had to be a plane. Being placed on ECMO at the Med Center meant he would be traveling with a lot of attachments plus medical personnel. A helicopter would not have had enough room to accommodate all of it. She also learned that even though ECMO was attached at the Johnson City

Medical Center, it could not be maintained there. It was a life support to get Johnny to Vanderbilt. He was taken by ambulance to the airport and transferred to a fixed-wing plane – a single-prop, six-seater.

A vision of the Call Center swept through her mind again. She remembered one nurse in particular that she worked with there. She was a strong Christian woman who would always personally pray for patients and family after transfer arrangements were made. She wondered if it was that nurse who made their arrangements. She would never know, of course, as everything that went on there was kept confidential. But she did wonder.

Right now, however, it was Christmas night and Johnny was finally on his way to Vanderbilt. Claudia, Sasha and Chris stopped home briefly to pack some clothes and headed west – Sasha driving Claudia's car and Chris leading the way in their car. Joshua and Jennifer went home to make arrangements for their children and their jobs and would soon follow. Hopes were high that this was the beginning of the next step in Johnny's healing.

In the Care of Friends and Strangers

It was only out of necessity that Claudia had to set aside her role as caregiver for her mother, Gerry. Her sudden and immediate need to be with Johnny dictated that she place Gerry's care into the hands of others.

Claudia and Johnny and her mother and father combined their homes in 2010. Her father, Richard, had been very ill and in and out of the hospital several times. Her mother, Gerry, was struggling with her own medical issues and did not feel that she could give him the care he needed at home by herself. Claudia knew – and Johnny agreed, that it was time for them to become her parents' caregivers.

Not wanting to move in with her parents, Johnny and Claudia started looking for a "together home" or, as most people would call it, one with a "mother-in-law apartment." They looked at many and fell in love with their present-day home in Jonesborough, Tennessee. It was everything they needed. It had a large three-bay garage and shed in the back with a full loft – enough for their cars and Richard's and Johnny's tools. The inside of the house was just as amenable. The laundry room separated her parent's bedroom and the kitchen from the rest of the home, providing easy access to Gerry and Richard in times of need while maintaining privacy for both families.

Even though his physical condition had deteriorated, Richard never gave up the hope that he would be able to work with his tools again someday. Claudia and Johnny did not take that hope away. When he wasn't in the hospital, he would take his walker and slowly cross the driveway, inch by inch, until he reached the garage and his tool box. Once there, he would pick up one tool at a time and put it in the basket on his walker and slowly return to where he intended to use it. One day, Claudia found him in the yard, lying on his back with his feet up in the air, kind of like an overturned turtle. He had fallen and was unable to turn himself over so he could get up. He just stayed there, waiting for someone to find him.

When Richard fell, Claudia and Johnny were there; when he had to go to the hospital, they were there. Richard was eventually placed in a nursing home where he resided until his passing in 2013.

***

During this time, Claudia worked twelve-hour night shifts at her nursing job at the Call Center, mainly coordinating the transfer of patients between hospitals. Then she would come home and take her parents to doctor appointments or wherever they needed to be before it was her time to retire and get some bed rest.

When her father was admitted to the nursing home, her personal schedule changed. She would go directly to the nursing home after her Call Center night shift and stay with him until the doctor made his rounds or until she could get a report from the nurses. In a positive way, it was their special father-daughter time together; but sometimes sleep won out over visiting. There were days when she was so exhausted, it just felt good to lay a pillow down on the side of her father's bed or on the bedside table and sleep. Usually by mid-morning she would drive home and take care of her mother's needs, then sleep until it was time to get ready for her next shift.

It was also during this time that Claudia met Jan Magee, a woman who would soon become a very special friend. She was a hospice nurse and they actually met for the first time at a Sisters of Faith meeting. Both being nurses, they struck up a conversation and friendship that would create a bond they never could have anticipated. The second time they met was at the nursing home where Claudia was visiting her dad and Jan happened to be there as well seeing her hospice patients.

"What are you doing here?" Jan asked at their chance meeting in the hallway.

"My father is a resident here," Claudia explained.

Jan immediately went to his room and met him. They became buddies right from the start. He and Jan were both jokesters. She visited him every time she was in the facility, which was two or three times a week, and they laughed and cut up together when he was able. As time progressed and Richard's condition deteriorated, he was placed on hospice and Jan became his hospice nurse. When her patient and friend Richard passed away in March 2013, Jan attended the funeral and was invited to the Randolph house afterward as one of the family.

***

Claudia's mother Gerry did tolerably well during this time, but it wasn't long before she had to stop driving because of her confusion. Claudia became her full-time caregiver, taking her to appointments, helping her with grocery shopping, monitoring her medications, and tending to all her of needs.

"For her age, mom is doing very well," Claudia says today. "She will be 90 in November (2018). She stays in her apartment and colors most of the time. She has reached the point where she doesn't like to go out much, no more than she has to. Mom has had some rough times over the past two and a half years since being diagnosed with Lewy Body Dementia. Lewy Body is a disease associated with abnormal deposits of a protein in the brain. These deposits lead to problems with thinking, movement, behavior, and mood. Lewy Body is associated with delusions and hallucinations, both of which mom has experienced. She has been so scared at times the she has crawled into bed with me, putting Johnny out on the couch.

"Delusions can best be described as beliefs or impressions that are firmly maintained, despite being contradicted by what can be seen or generally accepted as reality. Mom saw fish swimming in her c-pap water reservoir. She spent months with "bugs" in her overhead fan. She described them in detail with both of us lying on the bed and her pointing at each one. She described their vivid colors. She heard them eating, saw babies coming in and out of the back of the bugs. They were long and segmented and crunched when they chewed. They had a door in the ceiling fan that they entered and exited. One night as we lay on her bed, I took pictures of the fan, printed them off, and showed them to her. She pointed out and described everything she saw on the paper, just like she told it to me. It was real to her and still is.

"Another time mom was walking to her bed in a dimly lit room and saw curtains billowing in front of her. She kept waving her hands to get them out of the way and she said she got her feet caught in them and fell. The curtains were not real, but the fall was. She sustained a cracked rib and multiple bruises. Another time as the two of them were lying on her bed, she said the curtains were billowing again. 'Can't you see them?' mom asked. I took my legs, swung them in the air, and pretended to catch the moving curtains. There were no curtains. Mom put her legs up in the air to catch them also. Here we were, lying side by side on her bed, swinging our legs in the air. I said, 'Mom, you are the only 88-year-old-woman I know who can get her legs that high in the air!' We both had a good laugh.

"Hallucinations, on the other hand, are a different story. They are seen *but not believed* by the person experiencing them. Mom saw bears outside her bedroom window and lots of other animals, but she knew they weren't real when they started walking through the bedroom wall. 'Bears can't walk through walls,' she said. Mom has pictures of her family on the walls in her bedroom and she sees their mouths move like they are speaking, but she never hears any voices. She knows this is not real.

"We now take her to Vanderbilt and the medications they prescribed have helped her tremendously. Vanderbilt has been a life saver for our whole family."

***

During Claudia's absence from home to be with Johnny, many people stepped in to take care of Gerry – family members, friends, and even "strangers." While Claudia, Joshua and Jennifer, and Sasha and Chris were with Johnny, Claudia's son, Micah, traveled to Jonesborough from his home in Newport News, Virginia to help with Gerry's care and do things that needed to be done around the house.

Church friends and neighbors were there. Although dozens of people from church knew Gerry by association with Claudia as her mother, Gerry did not know *them* – not really. But their church family became a strong support group. One person, Tami, organized a food chain to make sure Gerry had food and companionship every day. They kept it going the entire time Claudia was with Johnny. They knocked on her door with a constant flow of dinners, flowers, and other niceties and, whether Gerry knew them well, somewhat, or not at all, they were welcomed with a smile and an invitation to come in and stay a while. Some did; others preferred a short, casual drop-by. While they were there, they made sure her phone and life alert were charged and medications were filled. Several SOF members even stayed overnight on occasion. But even with a confused mind, Gerry was aware of the reality that Johnny was sick and her daughter needed to be with him. By nature, she was gracious, hospitable, appreciative, and a model of perseverance.

***

Also left to the care of others were Claudia's dogs – all seven of them plus Johnny's lab mix pound dog, Beau.

"I am a breeder of Cavalier King Charles Spaniels, and my Kennel is best known as Rogan Cavaliers," Claudia explains. "A dear friend and owner of Camp Bowwow Kennel in Johnson City came to the rescue for our dogs when Johnny got sick. She was also my teacher and mentor when I first started showing Cavaliers. When she heard of Johnny's condition and found out we were in Nashville, she and her daughter came out and picked up all eight of our dogs, transported them in crates in the back of their cars, and kept them for us. Little did they know it was going to be for almost three months. They never put a time limit on their care; they just did what needed to be done and we took it day by day.

"I had just purchased another puppy and only had it four days when all this occurred with Johnny. By the time we saw the puppy again, she had been nurtured and was well on her way to being housebroken and socialized.

"She also sent my last puppy from a litter we had before Christmas to its forever home on New Year's Eve. It went to Alaska, with its forever parents coming all the way to Tennessee to pick her up by plane.

"When I was finally able to retrieve my dogs and tried to pay her, she adamantly refused to take my money. Instead, we just stood in her driveway and she gave me a hug. But I felt that I had to do *something* for her. I started ordering dog food and having it delivered to her front porch until she finally said, 'I have enough for the next year. Don't send me anymore!'

"Another friend, neighbor, and owner of four Cavaliers stepped in toward the end of our journey to supervise my returning fur babies and took over the care of the new puppy that I barely had a chance to get to know. She also checked on my mother as needed, sometimes sitting and talking with her and just keeping her company.

"Then there was a third friend who stepped in when needed, checking on and feeding the Cavaliers and Beau. Such great friends!

During all this time, our dogs had lots of attention and love. I never had to worry about them for a minute; it took a huge load off of my mind."

JOHNNY COME BACK

Settling into Nashville

The four-and-a-half-hour drive from Johnson City to Nashville gave Claudia a little time to sleep. They arrived at Vanderbilt just as hospital personnel were finishing up getting Johnny settled in from the plane ride. There were machines on both sides of the bed and IV poles hung in rows with 4-5 drips of medications on each row. The medications regulated every function of his body – blood pressure, insulin, thinning of the blood so the life support wouldn't clog, and a separate machine for continuous dialysis. There was a nurse who stayed at his bedside for her entire twelve-hour shift. If the nurse had to leave for any reason, another nurse stepped in. A second nurse who specialized in ECMO, the heart and lung support system that Johnny arrived with from the Johnson City Med Center, sat at the door continuously. Johnny was so closely monitored that Claudia felt like she could finally relax a little bit.

Sasha and Chris made a hotel reservation for the three of them for the first night, arriving very late (actually early morning). As they sat around the breakfast table the next day, Sasha and Chris found an extended stay hotel for Claudia. They debated whether to make a reservation on a day-to-day basis or longer. It would depend on what happened with Johnny. They finally decided to make it for a week, ending on January 2nd, with faith that Johnny was going to live! Sasha and Chris made it a Christmas present for Claudia – a rather unique gift, but very much appreciated! It was roomy enough that Johnny's children, Joshua and Jennifer, would be able to stay there with her when they arrived.

It was not only roomy but comfortable, complete with kitchenette and a nearby laundry room. Everyone pitched in and just did what needed to be done to make the most of the time they would be in Nashville. They made a trip to the local grocery store and stocked up on enough food for at least a week. Jennifer did the laundry for everyone. Johnny's niece, Susan, sent them a "care" package with dozens of items they would most likely need during their stay but hadn't thought of. Susan was also a nurse so she knew what was going to be needed. There was a room darkening mask used for the day sleepers (and for Johnny when he first started being able to open his eyes and the light irritated him), paper plates, paper towels, eating utensils, snacks, toothbrushes and toothpaste, deodorant, Benadryl®, ibuprofen, aspirin, individual flavored packs for bottled water, etc. It was another blessing for the trio tending to the bedside watch.

They took shifts staying with Johnny – Claudia during the day so she could talk with the physicians, Jennifer and Joshua sharing the night watches. Most of the time, however, the "shifts" didn't end. They overlapped for many hours. No one wanted to leave Johnny's bedside, especially if a procedure was to be done or if they were waiting for a report.

A volley of trips between Nashville and Johnson City began for Joshua and Jennifer. They left December 31st to go back home, with Joshua returning the next day with Claudia's other car and more items from the house that Sasha packed from a long list Claudia provided. The second car was needed so Joshua and Claudia could come and go as needed.

Jennifer returned on the 2nd with Joshua's truck. She was only able to stay a few days and had to return home to take care of their children, Emma and JJ. But Emma came down with the flu and Jennifer was not able to return to Vanderbilt. No one could be around Johnny or even in the hospital with any illness, especially the flu. It was weeks before Jennifer was able to see her father again.

Meeting Solomon

Tuesday, December 26

Claudia met Solomon on their first full day at Vanderbilt. It was a day of thankfulness mixed with anxiety. The surgery on Christmas Day was successful in that the ECMO kept Johnny alive; he was able to make the flight to Nashville with a stabilized heart and he still had his leg. But his condition was still tentative at best and the stress of the last few days had taken its toll on Claudia. She was still on top of anything that had to do with Johnny's care, of course, but silently would have welcomed someone to lean on – a strong person who truly understood the severity of Johnny's condition; someone who would be close at hand. That person was Solomon.

"Have you met Solomon?" Johnny's nurse, Trene, asked her.

"No, I haven't," replied a weary Claudia.

"Well, you must meet him. He is a Respiratory Therapist and will be working with Johnny."

Solomon was a big, jovial man with a smile on his face all the time – a spiritual up-lifter who spent a lot of time in Johnny's room. Still on the ventilator and ECMO, Johnny was kept in a deep sedation – as deep as they could go. Solomon was responsible for maintaining the airway of the ventilator, keeping Johnny suctioned, and giving treatments as directed by the physicians. It didn't take Claudia long to realize he was the strong person she needed in her corner. They quickly became friends. She even looked up the name "Solomon" because he meant so much to her, and discovered his name means peace.

Talking to Solomon did bring her peace, just like his name predicted. She told him about all the challenges they had experienced and overcome so far, especially because of the right people being in the right place at just the right time. She told him about her friend, Joy, whom she had not seen in years and who just happened to be on duty that night and her intervention when they first arrived at the Johnson City Medical Center. Then there was the nurse who handed Johnny's chart to a cardio-thoracic surgeon in the ICU – the one person who was really able to help their seemingly impossible situation. Yes, Solomon knew all about the plans that had to be in place to fly someone to Vanderbilt. He understood her concerns and her feelings and, most of all, he understood what Johnny needed as his body struggled to recover. Not only did Solomon provide a sense of peace as he listened and talked with Claudia, he was a person of very strong faith.

A few days after arriving at Vanderbilt, Claudia was going through a particularly gloomy time as doctors continued to try to keep Johnny stable while identifying his underlying health problems. The whole ordeal was becoming overwhelming, even to a seasoned nurse. "What are Johnny's chances?" she asked a physician. "What are we looking at?" As a nurse, these were questions she herself had heard so many times in the past from family members of patients she cared for. She knew there were no real answers; they just seemed like questions of hope.

"It doesn't look good," the physician replied. "Your husband is a very sick man."

His answer was painfully honest...which was fine. She wanted honest answers. But the truth still hurt her already heavy heart. When the physician left, Solomon came over and put his arm around her.

"I heard you talking to the doctor," he said with a reassuring smile, "but you were talking to the wrong physician."

Claudia immediately knew what he meant: God is the Great Physician – the real healer. She knew Solomon was right and it was what she needed to hear. It was not a question of hope; it was a question of faith. She never again asked another doctor what Johnny's chances were.

But she did think about what the doctor said: "Your husband is a very sick man." It was the day that "sick" took on a whole different meaning for her. She had heard that comment so many times in the last few days that she was on the verge of total frustration... until she realized that the word "sick" had a totally different meaning to these doctors than it always had to her as a nurse.

Being an Emergency Department nurse, she saw a lot of "sick" people over the years. She thought about it...people call in "sick" for work. I'm sick; I have a cold. I'm sick; I have a stomach ache. I'm sick.

Suddenly, she was seeing a different picture. When these doctors used the phrase "he is a sick man," it meant the whole body, every organ, every ounce of him was "sick." It described someone who was at the end. By the time she would leave Vanderbilt, Claudia would appreciate very well the difference in the measurement of "sick" from her nurse's standpoint and the perspective of the doctors who treat serious illnesses. As a nurse, she had always used the word "critical" to describe someone in Johnny's condition – someone who was past "sick." But at Vanderbilt, all the patients were critically ill when they arrived. Here, "sick" was past the critical stage. It was an adjustment for her.

A couple days later, she heard two physicians talking over at the side of the room, and she inadvertently *did* hear the answer to her previous question. One said, "If he makes it another twenty-four hours, he should have a fifty-fifty chance." It was another awakening. She had been thinking positive – along the lines of how far they had to go before Johnny was on the path to recovery, not the possibility of his dying. Twenty-four hours. It gave her chills. Once again, Solomon proved to be the rock she could lean on, assuring her that God was still in control. He later told her that when he went home that night, he mentioned to his wife he was taking care of a very sick man and together they prayed for Johnny and Claudia and their family.

Solomon was also a liaison with doctors. Months later, she would learn about a conversation he had with one of the physicians as they were standing by the machines that were keeping Johnny alive:

"There is no reason for him to be alive or to make it, scientifically speaking or on paper" the physician said. "It's just not possible."

But Solomon, knowing how totally Claudia was immersed in her husband's care and how hard she was praying, sometimes by herself with her head bowed, other times while leaning over her husband, responded: "You see that woman over there praying over him with all her faith? With her faith, he <u>will</u> make it."

"We'll see," the physician said.

Faith! That single word meant so much to Claudia right now. She never knew how deep her faith was until it was tested day after day. She now relied totally on her faith in God and faith that He was guiding the wisdom and hands of the doctors. She acknowledged each day that Johnny was alive as a miracle. One of her favorite scriptures was now a life line:

Hebrews 11:1: "Faith is the substance of things hoped for, the evidence of things not seen."

The Haven

Claudia's one-week reservation at the extended-stay hotel would be up January 2nd, a couple days away. When they first arrived in Nashville, there was no way of knowing how long they would be there. Days? Weeks? It was only a guess. Sasha and Chris made the reservation for one week, based on the hope that Johnny would be getting better or at least hold his own and they could better estimate a departure date. Now they knew there was no way he was going to be going home any time soon. Claudia needed to think about renewing – not one day at a time, but one week at a time.

While sitting in ICU with Johnny that day, she thought about a lot of things – how the old year was going out, what the new year held in store. She thought about all the ways people celebrated a new year – parties, food, music, noise makers, fireworks. All she wanted was to have her husband back, a quiet word, a look of recognition...that was all. Instead, she was sitting by his bedside in an out-of-town hospital, thinking about a hotel room without him.

She allowed her mind to drift back to the ushering in of new years past. Sometimes it was just the two of them; sometimes it was with family or friends. A new year was always a time for reminiscing and memories, but never like this.

She pushed it all out of her mind. It was time to face the moment and the realities at hand! Where to stay was the next thing she had to tackle and soon. *Should I stay where I am? That would be the easiest thing to do, but it is a little pricey. Maybe there is something nearby that would be more reasonable. I will make some calls tomorrow.*

Before she could make her first call, one of Jennifer's work friends contacted her on Facebook Messenger and told her about a Church in Nashville that had a house they used for situations like theirs and gave her a telephone number. "There have been several families from Johnson City who have stayed there in the past," the message said, but there was no indication that the house was available; the information was just being passed along for whatever use it might be. *It is certainly worth a call,* Claudia decided as she tapped the number into her phone the next morning.

A woman named Donna answered, identifying herself as a caretaker of the home called "The Haven." Donna told her they had been remodeling The Haven but it was not quite finished. Plus, there were a couple of people on a waiting list ahead of her. Even though it was not the answer Claudia hoped for, Donna was such a friendly person that they started talking about Johnny's illness and all that had happened. Claudia told her about the blessings – yes, even "miracles" they had experienced so far and her faith that God was with them and would pull her husband through this crisis. It was an unexpected conversation with a caring, Christian person and, in the midst of all that was going on with Johnny, it felt so good! Even though it couldn't work out, it just felt good to talk! She still had a couple of days to look into other options but, if nothing more reasonable came along, she would just stay where she was, renewing weekly, and juggling the expenses as best she could.

Donna called back the next day. "I've been praying about you," she told Claudia. "I believe God wants you to have this house. It will be ready for you to move in on *Tuesday, January 2nd!*

The Haven was aptly named. It was not a big place, but it was more than big enough to accommodate Claudia and her family. It became *their* haven and it was love at first sight or, as Claudia describes it, "It just wrapped its arms around me!"

When they arrived on moving-in day, Claudia and Joshua spent time walking around, admiring the verses on the wall, and enjoying pictures of people who had been there previously along with pictures of their loved ones. Claudia made a mental note to have a picture of Johnny made to include on the wall, and added Donna to her texting prayer list. Donna became another special friend.

The Haven was an amazing place. It was far more than they ever expected or could even have imagined. The kitchen was fully stocked, not only with dishes and cooking utensils, but the cabinets were full of food for them. The refrigerator was stocked with sausage, eggs, milk, luncheon meats and cheeses. The children from Donna's church collected their change and put it in a jar at The Haven for them to use for snacks in vending machines at the hospital. The bathroom had all the essential toiletries in case they forgot something. Everything they could possibly need was provided for them except for a washer and dryer, and that was only because the basement had not been finished yet; it would be available for the next family. Their only expense was the electric bill at a mere $6 a day. "The Haven" was truly a blessing!

***

A trip to the laundromat was something Claudia had not experienced for years and it turned out to be another technological challenge, just like her new smart phone. The machines were commercial models, of course, with instructions and coin slots everywhere. It took a while, but she finally figured out how to operate the washer. While it was working away, she sat quietly near the window, thinking about Johnny...and watching it snow! She was hoping there would not be much of an accumulation because she was on her way to Vanderbilt – about twenty minutes from the laundromat if she didn't get lost. That thought made her smile. *I do get lost a lot*, she admitted to herself. *My GPS never seems to take me along the same route twice. It must have some kind of high-tech sense of humor, knowing I am directionally challenged.*

When she looked back toward her washing machine, she noticed a small, middle-aged woman washing sleeping bags and wondered if she was homeless. *She looks like a meth person with sores on her face and arms and very thin,* she analyzed as she turned back to the window.

Claudia took her clothes out of the washer, put them in the dryer, and fed her coins into a slot, but the machine wouldn't run. She read the instructions again, checked the settings, and pushed more buttons, but the dryer just sat there. *What am I doing wrong?*

42

Must be something, but what? she asked herself with annoyance. *I've done everything it says to do!*

She needed help. Hesitantly, she approached the other woman who obligingly came over to help determine the problem. To Claudia's chagrin, she had put her coins into the wrong slot, actually adding extra time to the other woman's dryer rather than her own. But it worked out alright. "My sleeping bags are just about finished," the woman said, "and you can just move your clothes to my dryer."

While they waited for the clothes to dry, they struck up a conversation about the accumulating snow, Johnny, and the Goodwill Center down the street where the woman worked. She must have sensed Claudia's concern over the snow and told her who to call in case there was a power outage. "Wherever you are staying, make sure you have a flashlight and extra batteries," she smiled. It made Claudia wonder if The Haven had a flashlight, where it would be, and if the batteries were still good. She made a mental note to check it out when she got back to the Haven.

"Thank you for all the good information," Claudia said thankfully. "It is so helpful to a new person in town." Silently, as she looked at the sleeping bags the woman was rolling up, however, she still wondered if the woman was homeless.

The conversation continued while clothes were being folded and Claudia moved her load of laundry from one machine to the other. It was mostly about Johnny, the struggles and solutions that had already taken place, and the one miracle they were still waiting for – Johnny being completely healed.

Claudia's phone rang just as the woman was preparing to leave. With basket in hand, she came over to Claudia, standing back respectfully while she was still on the phone, waiting until she ended her conversation. Then she added, "I just want you to know that I will be praying for you."

It was another chance encounter that Claudia will never forget. "I felt so ashamed of myself for judging her like I did and shying away. I was humbled. Many more things would humble me over the next few months. I was taken to my knees so many times."

Highs and Lows at Vanderbilt

Johnny remained on ECMO and sedated for the first six days at Vanderbilt. As ECMO was controlling all of his body's vital functions, the only way of knowing how he was doing was by lab values and testing of the heart by echocardiograms (a diagnostic test that uses ultrasound waves to create an image of the heart muscle. Echo waves rebound off the heart and show size, shape, and movement of the heart muscle). The lab tests did not look very promising, but the echocardiograms eventually did show slight improvement. Normal values for a blood ejection rate are 55-60%; Johnny's were between 10-20%. Although the heart was recovering, scientifically and on paper, he should not have been alive. The kidneys were not recovering and he was still on dialysis. The liver functions were not worsening at this point and may even have had a small amount of improvement.

On December 29th, while Johnny was still sedated and on ECMO, a heart catherization (procedure to diagnose and treat cardiovascular conditions) was done with a biopsy of the heart muscle tissue to determine the possible cause of Johnny's myocarditis. The biopsy confirmed viral myocarditis, but the cause remained elusive. He was also tested again for the possibility of cytomegalovirus (CMV). His CMV level at Johnson City Medical Center had not detected any of the virus; the blood test at Vanderbilt showed he had a low level of the virus in his system but the biopsy did not show any CMV.

Note: An explanation of testing for the presence of CMV is that the level of CMV in the blood can vary depending on when the test is taken. The actual level of the virus in the blood rises and falls, so it would be hard to determine at what point during the cycle the blood was drawn. If not drawn when the virus level was high, it could be missed. Although CMV testing at Vanderbilt did indicate a low level, there remained doubts among some of the physicians that Johnny's condition was being impacted by CMV.

***

While Johnny's vital signs didn't fluctuate with the ECMO system sustaining him, Claudia knew he was declining. She just felt it. During one of their bleakest moments, when Johnny's life was hanging by a mere thread to his worldly body, Claudia leaned over him, talked quietly into his ear, crying and begging him: "Johnny, please don't leave me. Johnny, come back to me. Don't leave me, Johnny. Come back." She laid her head on his chest, letting the tears run down her cheek onto his bare chest. "Johnny, come back to me!' she kept repeating. It was her scariest and weakest moment. She prayed without ceasing, "Johnny, please come back. Come back to me."

Johnny later told her that he had heard her voice. He said he could see a light for a while but it was fading out and things had gotten real dark...but something stronger than the darkness said he just couldn't leave Claudia, his children and grandchildren. He heard her voice through the darkness, reading the bible and the texts of prayers from the Sisters of Faith. He heard her praying over him and talking to him. He knew he had to come back. Then the darkness started to leave.

During this time, Johnny's son Joshua was over in the corner of the room on his knees with his head bowed, praying for his father.

"How humbling for him and how proud Johnny would be," Claudia remembered thinking as she watched him.

For a touch of humor, Claudia added with a smile, "Johnny loves watching Westerns and I don't. This has always been a bit of a battle in our house. I promised Johnny he could watch all the Westerns he wanted if he would come back to me and I would never say a word. He doesn't remember hearing me say that but, to this day, I have kept my promise."

Another scary time while Johnny was on the ECMO machine was when there was a malfunction and the machine stopped. It was around midnight and alarms went off everywhere. Before Claudia even realized what was happening, there were more than a dozen responders at the door and in the room. While they were working with the machine, his physician stood there, alert to everything and everyone around him. "They were like a fine-tuned machine working together," Claudia recalled. "The concern was that because his blood had been circulating and was now stopped, it may clot and not be able to run through the machine. Johnny would be denied his life saving blood from re-entering his body and his heart would not be pumping. They were in a time crunch – a short one, to find the problem and fix it. They worked fast and hard... many hands trying to figure out what had happened. I don't remember the cause, but it was fixed very quickly and all the machines started their rhythmic beating again. If they had not found the problem, Johnny would not have come back to me. If the machine doesn't run, the patient doesn't live. Plain and simple, no alternatives. As my friend, Joy, had pointed out to me, ECMO was his last and only chance of survival.

"To keep the blood thin enough to go through the machine without clotting," she continued to explain, "he was on a blood thinner – Heparin®. It had to stay thin for the machine to run. It was crucial to not have clots plugging the filter that the blood went through. If there were clots going through the body, the side effect of this could be a brain bleed or stroke or pulmonary embolism (a blood clot in the lung).

"It was December 30th when the doctors started bringing Johnny out of the induced coma. They would bring him out a little more each day and let him rest in between. It was a slow process, all the while continually checking him for neuro deficits or stroke. When he first started to wake up, he was not responding to any commands. The doctors were not concerned, explaining that this happens sometimes when they first try to wake a patient up after being sedated as deeply as he had been. He was reassessed every few hours. They checked for his ability to move his fingers and toes. Can you feel this? Is it sharp or dull? The first time he moved after being weaned off sedation was when I was repeatedly calling his name. He turned his head in my direction with his eyes still closed. It had been a long time, but he finally turned toward my voice. It was an awesome moment! I was cautioned that there was a possibility he may have deficits after all he had gone through and only time would tell, but I knew better. I remember thinking...and perhaps I even said it out loud: You don't know how much God has already brought us through, and you don't know my Johnny. He can do this!"

Claudia sent a progress report via text message to her new friend Donna, overseer of The Haven. "Thank you for the update," she texted back. "Continuing to pray."

"When Johnny finally did respond to grip and movement," Claudia continues, "it was determined that his right side was weaker than the left. There was concern about a possible stroke because of the blood thinners he had been on for ECMO. He was sent to CT for a head scan and all was clear. Great news!"

Sunday, December 31

On New Year's Eve day, Johnny finally came off ECMO, the temporary life-saving support system he had been on since Christmas Day. His heart was strong enough to sustain him without mechanical assistance, although he remained sedated and on the ventilator to support his lungs. But he was still "sick" and remained in Cardiac ICU.

One of the issues was severe diarrhea which Johnny had since his second day at Vanderbilt. It was copious, nothing like Claudia had ever seen as a nurse.

Another issue was ulcerations (severe abrasion) of his mouth. Although medical personnel provided thorough mouth care, he had developed sores and scabs in his mouth and down his throat. Pieces of the tip of his tongue were eaten away. Places in the middle of his tongue developed divots or fissures.

Both of these conditions continued to worsen, which was not normal just from intubation. They were both indicators of CMV. Infectious Disease was consulted and another CMV titer was drawn. **An elevation of the virus was detected.** Johnny was started on antiviral medication. Within twenty-four hours, there was a significant turn-around in his condition. The antibiotics he had been on were stopped and he continued to improve.

New Year's Eve was celebrated in a very different way this year – with the "turn team." It consisted of three or four people who came into the room every two hours to turn Johnny from side to side to back to help with preserving his skin integrity. They were there at 10:00 p.m. and said, "See you at midnight and we can celebrate the new year while turning him." They were always upbeat, smiling, and a comfort for the family.

Wednesday, January 3

January 3rd began another scary episode that was quickly developing into a nightmare. With Johnny still under sedation because of the ventilator, he could not be extubated (have his breathing tube removed) until he could breathe on his own. The doctors didn't want to leave him on the ventilator any longer as it could lead to additional medical complications, including pneumonia. But the weaning-off process was not going well at all! He continued to have trouble breathing. They decided that the best answer was to do a tracheotomy (a surgical procedure of cutting into the trachea through the neck to allow the passage of air). This would leave him with a tracheostomy (a surgical formation of an opening into the trachea through the neck). Claudia said no! Johnny would not want that!

As a nurse, she was very familiar with the consequences of leaving a breathing tube in too long. She was very familiar with the tracheotomy procedure as well as the tracheostomy. She also knew there was no guarantee that it could be reversed at some time in the future. Often it was not. She envisioned her husband at home, suctioning and cleaning, and all the medical problems associated with it, including an increased chance of pneumonia and infections. No, she knew Johnny wouldn't want that!

"He is much more likely to get pneumonia if we leave it in any longer," they argued.

She knew this was true. The doctors already told her his chest x-ray showed possible signs of pneumonia. The update she sent out that day included prayer requests for Johnny that he did not have pneumonia and also wisdom for herself for the serious decision she had to make.

The test came back the next day that Johnny did <u>not</u> have pneumonia *at that time*.

She remained steadfast in refusing to sign the consent papers for a tracheotomy. It wasn't because she wanted to be difficult, but because she knew her husband. She knew his deep-down inner strength and knew he could do this! He had already overcome so many obstacles that were worse. She also knew that the physicians and nurses were getting frustrated with her and she didn't want that either.

"We have come too far not to do this for him," they told her. "We can't let this happen. It would be dangerous...life-threatening. Do you have grandchildren? Don't you want to see him ten years from now on Christmas morning playing with them?"

What a guilt trip! But she held her ground and kept praying for an answer. There was nothing...no clear indication as to what she should do. Time was running out. She finally gave in on the third evening, consented, and signed the papers to have the trach done the next morning. She was still feeling guilty about signing the consent, knowing that Johnny's quality of life would change. And depending on the outcome.... well she didn't even want to think about it; she just didn't know! *God works in mysterious ways,* she kept reminding herself. *It is His timing, not mine.*

Later that evening, Johnny's respiratory therapist found an obstruction in the tube that was hindering his breathing and they had to replace the tube. While they did that, they went on down into the lungs and cultured the fluids for any sign of infection and cleaned out the excess secretions. The cultures were clear; no infection in the lungs. Claudia's hopes rose, thinking that the obstruction might have been the problem or at least part of it, but the papers had already been signed to do the surgical procedure. The trach team was scheduled to arrive at 9 a.m.

"Please, please, please!" a determined Claudia pleaded with the doctor late that night. "Can't we try one more time?" She knew that replacing the tube had all the possibilities of clearing the lungs and making it easier for him to breathe.

"Yes," the doctor relented. "We will try one more time." Claudia felt as though he was pacifying her, but she didn't care. He said they would let him rest through the night and try weaning him off the ventilator again at 6 a.m.

The night was filled with hope, text messages, prayers, and anticipation. At 6 a.m. on January 4th, Johnny was taken off the ventilator one more time. Gradually...but steadily, he began breathing on his own. The doctor said he had to remain breathing on his own until 9 a.m.

Claudia was on an emotional roller coaster. The fact that Johnny was starting to breathe on his own sent her adrenalin into high gear, but she didn't want to tell anyone until she knew for sure that he was going to make it. She waited a little while...and started thinking: *If I wait to see if he will continue to breathe on his own before I tell anyone, then I am doubting God. Do I have unwavering faith or don't I?* She texted everyone to let them know he was off the ventilator. No exceptions. No "wait and sees". It was plain and simple: Johnny is off the ventilator!

At 9 a.m., as scheduled, the trach team arrived at the door. The doctor's words were beautiful music to her ears: "You can go now; it looks like we don't need you. I'll call you later if the situation changes." Claudia almost collapsed with exhaustion and relief. She never saw the trach team again.

A day or two later, as Claudia walked past the nurses' station, one of the physicians – the one who had insisted that Johnny needed the trach, was sitting there and stopped her. "You made a liar out of me," he commented jokingly but serious.

"I had a good physician," she replied, and pointed toward Heaven.

His quizzical look gave way to a smile when he realized what she meant. Claudia walked away with a smile also – on her face and in her heart. She knew the physician had been privileged to share one of their miracles. Something happened that, as a physician, he had not expected, but through faith, <u>she</u> had.

Still texting with Donna from The Haven: "Johnny is off the ventilator and no trach. Our new hope is for kidney functions to return. I believe in whole healing of the body."

Donna's reply: "Am in complete agreement and continuing to pray for you both."

"We are delighted with the house; it is so peaceful there," Claudia texted again.

Donna replied with a verse:

"Fear not, for I am with you. Be not dismayed, for I am your God. I will strengthen you, yes I will help you, I will uphold you with my righteous right hand." Isaiah 41:10."

She stood over Johnny and read it to him. She never erased any of the text messages with Bible verses and notes of inspiration from family and friends. She read them to Johnny over and over again, especially when she was praying "Come back to me!"

***

After being removed from ECMO, sedation, the ventilator, and the breathing tube, Johnny's next hurdle was movement. He had lost all of his muscle tone and strength. He was so weak he could not raise his arms, move his legs, or touch his face. Movement of any kind was totally dependent on those around him. But he could talk and his head was clear. He decided he wanted Claudia to lay down beside him. He kept saying "Come lay down with me, come lay down with me." Of course, she wanted to – it would be so comforting for both of them, but there were lines and tubes everywhere! There was no room for a second body on that bed.

The nurse encouraged her. "Go on," she said. "I'll help you."

She moved carefully under the lines and tubes and got over near him. Johnny was totally immobile. She picked his arm up and crawled into his arms. It just flopped down over her and he couldn't pick up the other arm to hold her. She tried to pull his arm around her but it was too heavy, just dead weight. Claudia got amused and said, "This just isn't going to work!," laughed, and got up.

Johnny's son Joshua was in the room and chimed in: "Do I need to leave?" They all got a chuckle out of it. It felt so good to laugh! Unfortunately, Johnny would never be able to join in the humor of that time as he would never remember it.

While all this was going on, Johnny was dealing with yet another problem ever since Christmas Eve back in Johnson City. His heart was going in and out of atrial fibrillation and flutter. Atrial fibrillation is a quivering or irregular heartbeat (arrhythmia) that can lead to heart-related complications. Atrial flutter results from an abnormal circuit inside the right atrium, or upper chamber of the heart. It beats extra-fast, at times up to 250-400 beats per minute. A normal heartbeat is 60-100 beats per minute. The two rhythms (atrial fibrillation and atrial flutter) sometimes alternate back and forth and this was happening with Johnny. The main danger is that the heart doesn't pump blood very well when it beats too fast. Vital organs like the heart muscle and brain may not get enough blood, which can cause them to fail. Congestive heart failure, heart attack, and stroke all can result.

Because of these rhythms, it was decided that Johnny needed to be cardioverted – a procedure by which an abnormally fast heart rate or other cardiac arrhythmia is converted to a normal rhythm using electricity or drugs. They used electricity with Johnny. Claudia sat in the corner of the ICU room and watched as they placed the paddles on his chest and shocked him. She knew what to expect because she had done this on patients herself in the ER, but it still hurt to see her husband's chest jump off the bed from the electrical current. The physicians did it once and nothing happened. It was repeated, this time with success. He went back into a normal rhythm. It did not last long, however, and was repeated again without success.

They did this procedure a couple of different times on other days, without success, and eventually agreed among themselves not to try cardioverting again.

Saturday, January 6

Another problem he was dealing with was dialysis. After being removed from ECMO and *continuous* dialysis, Johnny was scheduled for hemodialysis three times a week – Tuesday, Thursday, and Saturday, starting on January 6. Hemodialysis is the procedure of filtering impurities from the blood when the kidneys are not able to do the job. The blood is circulated through a machine, the filter catches the impurities, and the blood is returned to the body. Johnny had to lie almost perfectly still for five hours each time. If he didn't lie still, the machines would go off and the nurses would have to readjust tubing. "When this happened, he felt bad, knowing he was the cause of their extra work," Claudia says. "That is so typical of Johnny, always thinking of someone other than himself.

"There are many changes that can occur in a person's body while having dialysis," she explains. "The fluid shifts can affect the heart. It is not uncommon for people to become hypotensive – low blood pressure from the fluids being removed. Johnny had a real problem with dialysis because he was already hypotensive. They were never able to draw more than half of what they needed to because his blood pressure dropped so low. He was a touch-and-go man a couple of times during dialysis.

"Johnny's heart rhythm was also affected by dialysis. Every time he had a treatment, he came back with a different heart rhythm and we never knew what rhythm he was going to have.

"He always felt terrible afterward and spent the time in between treatments dreading going back to dialysis again. Then one day he saw a young man appearing to be in his 20's having dialysis near him. It broke his heart knowing that the young man may go through dialysis for the rest of his life, with his only other hope being a kidney transplant. He still thinks about that young man.

"During one of Johnny's dialysis treatments, a nurse in the adjoining room kept watching us. She was short and petite with short brown hair, middle-aged. Johnny's nurse was a systemic nurse, monitoring the equipment but having little interaction with us. When Johnny's nurse left the room for a short time, the nurse in the adjoining room came over to his bedside. We assumed she was just checking on him since our nurse was gone."

"I don't know if you remember me," she said, "but I took care of your husband a couple of times when he was on ECMO in ICU."

"I felt really bad that I didn't remember her and apologized, but there were so many doctors and nurses, and all the different departments, and then the twelve-hour shifts. We met a lot of people.

"But she was so sweet and asked Johnny if she could pray for him. Of course, he said yes. She took his hand and prayed. Then she smiled, patted his hand, and quietly left the room. We never saw her again, but will never forget her. It was like having an encounter with an angel in disguise."

The consensus of the doctors regarding dialysis was pretty much the same: *He is in recovery. Only time will tell how well his kidneys recover. People his age rarely come off dialysis. His creatinine is high.* (Creatinine is a chemical waste product in the blood that passes through the kidneys to be filtered and eliminated in urine. A normal Creatinine level is 0.6-1.2; Johnny's was 7.5.) But he <u>was</u> in the recovery stage and his levels were checked daily.

<u>Tuesday, January 9</u>

Tuesday, January 9th, was "moving day!" After sixteen days in ICU, Johnny was transferred to the Heart Failure floor. It was a positive step forward! Claudia began staying in the room with him at night as well as during the day since Joshua and Jennifer had to return home and gave up their night shift.

"It was a tiny room," Claudia recalls. "They did eventually find me a cot, and this was the only time I had a cot throughout our stay at Vanderbilt. It had to be closed up during the day because you couldn't open the bathroom door when the cot was open. If I got up at night, I had to slide in sideways through the bathroom door. The bathroom itself was an icebox. They had remodeled some of the rooms, but this appeared to be an older part of the hospital. There was a piece of metal or something over an existing window. It was so cold!

"I wore jeans and layered sweaters every day inside the hospital, although the staff obligingly provided me with blankets and pillows and anything I asked for. When my cot was folded up during the day, the only place to put the blankets and pillows was over the wall heating and air system. There was a pile at least three and sometimes four feet high of sheets, pillows and blankets.

"This had become my home," Claudia recalled with a smile. "Johnny and I have a large home with plenty of space and we started joking about how well we were surviving in such small living quarters. We have always had a close relationship, but this experience has brought us even closer. Life is so precious!"

The consensus now was that the CMV virus <u>was</u> the major underlying cause of Johnny's heart condition. It had attacked his heart!

When Johnny was taken off high flow O2 oxygen that he had been on since being extubated from the ventilator, he was placed on regular oxygen tubing. It was the feeding tube, however, that was his worst enemy; he hated it. It was placed in the nose and went down to the stomach. It was so irritating on his throat and esophagus because of the scabs and sores left by the CMV virus. "No more, never again," he insisted. "Take it out." Although it was secured to the best of anyone's ability, Johnny was coughing so hard, trying to clear the debris from his throat and lungs, that he kept bringing the feeding tube back up. He coughed it out, they put it back. It was finally removed on January 10th, his second day on the Heart Failure floor...another positive step forward.

The antiviral medicine he had been put on was working. The diarrhea left, but it had already been around for more than two weeks into the stay at Vanderbilt. Combined with his weakened and malnourished condition, he developed huge and painful bed sores.

The mouth ulceration did not leave. The roof of his mouth remained rough, an ongoing condition that caused him to lose his sense of taste. Sweet now tasted sour. In order for food to have any real flavor at all, it had to have a lot of salt. This turned out not to be a problem since he was hypotensive (low blood pressure).

Johnny was told he would have to stay on the antiviral medication even after he left Vanderbilt – perhaps for months, while his heart and body continued to improve. He had to stay on it long enough **to make sure** *there was no CMV in three consecutive blood draws a couple of days apart.* But taking the medication proved to be a complication because of the dialysis. It had to be taken after the treatments for optimum results because if it were given before the treatment, all the medication would have been filtered out of his body. So he took it right after dialysis three times a week. It was not the preferred way of giving it, but it was the only way for Johnny.

Claudia did her research into the cost of the pills: $230 for ten of them. Once again, there was no alternative. It would be what it had to be. And once again, Claudia remained rooted in her faith that it would all work out... somehow.

Leaving Vanderbilt

January 15th was a good news/not-so-good news day. First, there was the prospect of finally being able to leave Vanderbilt...but with a long-term access for dialysis treatment. A tunnel catheter was placed (a designated port for dialysis only), with the anticipation that dialysis would be on-going. Johnny still had other lines that could be accessed for IV medications or in case of emergency treatment.

The next day – January 16th, was the scheduled day for departure. Leaving Vanderbilt after twenty-three days was exciting in one respect, but somewhat unnerving because of the winter weather. Johnny was to be transferred by ambulance to Quillen Rehabilitation Hospital in Johnson City, Tennessee, just a few miles from home. Claudia texted everyone and announced it on Facebook with big bold letters the good news that Johnny would soon be on his way home!

Early in the morning, however, the snow increased; road conditions worsened; snow was accumulating across the state. The ambulance personnel called and said they weren't going to be able to make the trip because of the roads. Claudia sent updated messages about the delay.

An hour later, they called back and said there was a window of clearing in the weather and they were going after all. The ambulance was on its way. The doctors came in to do their last rounds...but Claudia knew there were still a couple of unresolved issues. She reminded them that Johnny still had sutures in his lower leg from the fasciotomy that was done at the Johnson City Medical Center Christmas Day. There were three incisions in his lower leg that were made to relieve the pressure that had built up from the occluded veins in his leg.

There were also staples in his groins from the impella and ECMO. Being a nurse, she knew that they should be removed before Johnny was transported or it would be another issue at Quillen, the accepting facility. Otherwise, no one would know when they had been placed or when the surgeon(s) wanted them removed. That was the norm in dealing with sutures and transferred patients.

Claudia had been having ongoing conversations with the physicians about having them removed but there always seemed to be more pressing issues than sutures and staples. Vascular said the attending physicians could remove them and the attending physicians wanted Vascular to remove them. Now the time had suddenly come for him to be transferred and the sutures and staples still had not been removed.

NOW they were an issue! NOW it was 9:45 a.m. and EMS was at the door, ready to take Johnny to Quillen. They HAD to leave by 10:00 because of the weather. NOW they were rushing to get it done.

Johnny's groins had been draining for over two weeks – serious draining, with his dressings having to be changed two or three times a day. When the nurses brought it to the attention of the physicians at different times, they were given orders to keep them covered with a dressing. It was a "wait and see" situation.

When the staples were removed, everything broke open – big time, in both groins and two of the three incisions in his leg! Where the ECMO had been placed, the open wound was wide, two-and-a-half to three inches long, and two inches deep. They could see the vein pulsating. The incisions had not healed, most likely from all the steroids Johnny had been on.

Claudia had been posting announcements on Facebook – first, that they were going home. Then she posted the trip had been cancelled. Then she posted they were going and EMS was there. She was so sure it was going to happen. EMS was at the door! Those hopes were dashed when the doctor told EMS, "He is not going anywhere today." She learned not to jump the gun with public announcements. Everyone on Facebook was confused and the questions came in – was he coming home or wasn't he?

A culture was done on the wounds. The results showed Johnny had E coli – a bacterial infection, growing in his groin wounds. He was definitely not ready to be moved from Vanderbilt to Quillen Rehab.

Although disappointing, Claudia and Johnny both realized it was a good thing that the infection was discovered before trying to move him. He was not ready yet. Antibiotics were started.

Four wound vacs were placed: two in the lower leg and one in each groin. (Wound vacs consist of a granulation foam packed into the wounds with drains running from the wounds to a canister that operates by suction. They speed up the healing time of wounds, enabling them to heal from the inside out.) This was to be Johnny's new friend and side kick.

Looking ahead: He came back to Johnson City with the wound vacs and wore them 24/7 for almost two more months, until all the wounds had healed from the inside out. They were removed on May 11 by Home Health. That would be the date he was finally free of all attachments since the first line was placed on December 22, 2017.

It was two days later – January 18, when Johnny underwent one last dialysis treatment at Vanderbilt before being transferred. His hemoglobin had dropped to 5.1...the normal range is 12-15. He received a blood transfusion during his dialysis treatment and that brought his level up to 6. They felt this was sufficient enough for transfer.

While waiting for news regarding their departure and for Johnny to finish his treatment, Claudia called Helen Conger, an amazing 95-year-old lady from their church.

"Helen has been such a blessing to me since I first came to Jonesborough United Methodist Church nine or ten years ago," Claudia explains. "My affiliation with the church started as being the Parish Nurse. As responsibilities with my family grew, I had to resign as Parish Nurse, but my heart stayed in that church and we have attended there ever since. Our church has a Prayer Chain. Whenever there is a need for prayer, one phone call is made which sets off a series of calls to many people. Helen is a true Prayer Warrior and the person who would always call me. Then I would call the next person, and down the chain it goes. I just felt a need to make a call *to her* this time."

"I am so glad you called, Claudia!" exclaimed a delighted and sincere Helen Conger. "I have been thinking about you and I just want you to know that we are praying for you day and night. You have no idea how many people are praying for you. It is so cold here and I can't get out – four degrees last night, but I call and check on your mom every couple of days."

Just hearing Helen's voice was peaceful and reassuring as Claudia packed and prepared for the next phase of their journey – going home.

<u>Friday, January 19</u>

It happened at last! It was late morning and they were finally on their way to Quillen Rehab in Johnson City – Johnny by ambulance and Claudia not far behind in her car. The quiet time on the road gave her a chance to think about all that had transpired. She turned on the recording feature of her new smart phone, an updated version from her old phone that she had just learned how to use. She wanted to remember this moment...this time of uplifted spirits. Someday she might want to share her thoughts with others who needed to hear them. It was just a feeling she had.

"Johnny has already left by ambulance," she recorded. "He is in good spirits and I am in good spirits. I am just thinking about all that has happened since Christmas...the blessings and the joys that we have had, the ups and downs that we have had, and, most of all, the support we have had. Support has been incredible – from our family, our friends, our church people, and from people in churches across the country that we don't even know. I can't even imagine how many people have prayed for us. And those things are all important. But one of the most important things I have personally learned through this journey is about faith...my own faith. I never knew *really* how much faith I had; it's just not something you ever realize about yourself.

"I am not a person who just gets down on my knees and prays all the time. Often, I don't even know what to say when I do get ready to pray, but it is in my heart and I usually just say, "God, you know what I am feeling, and you know my innermost needs," or something along that line. And He does know, and I feel His presence. I have never doubted it. Praying, even without the 'right words,' has always brought me peace because I knew that whatever happened...whichever way things went, we would be okay.

"There were a couple of times when I really felt like we were losing Johnny – times when we probably didn't even realize how close we came because of the mechanical devices that were keeping him alive. But even when he was lying in that bed on the ECMO machine, he was a testimony himself just by his being there and still being alive. We knew, and everyone around us knew, that just the fact he had made it that far was a sheer miracle. He is known at the Johnson City Medical Center and Vanderbilt as The Christmas Miracle. Word travels fast in the medical field.

"Pray without ceasing. Have you ever heard that before? I have many times and never really knew what it meant. Actually, I had been doing it all my life and never knew that's what I was doing. It is the simple things I do without even realizing, but they remind me that God is with me and I am thanking Him. When I do something as commonplace as dropping something on the floor and it doesn't break, I spontaneously say "Thank you, God." When I am driving and late for an appointment and the light is green, I say "Thank you, God" as I go through it. When I read Facebook and people request prayer, I just put my hand over my computer screen and say, "Lord, take care of them." When I receive an email from our church requesting prayer, I lay my hand over the request and say, "You know what they need." It is as easy as that – everyday, simple things that show me I am praying without ceasing; nothing elaborate, but continuous. My subconscious is praying without ceasing.

LEAVING VANDERBILT

"Now we're leaving Vanderbilt and heading for rehab close to home. That in itself is a miracle – a big one! But we are so thankful for each and every miracle, big and small, not just the ones that sustained his life. There have been so many."

- - - - - - - - - - - - - - - - - -

Even though the trip from Vanderbilt to home was a time of hope that the ordeal was almost over, it was not. There would be much more ahead. But no matter what happened, they knew they were in God's hands. It was total trust and the source of their peace.

JOHNNY COME BACK

Rehab

The first morning at Quillen Rehab was a disaster! Johnny was scheduled for dialysis at 7:30 a.m. at DaVita Dialysis Center in Johnson City and would be transported by ambulance. However, the medical personnel at Quillen had no idea how "sick" he really was.

Two nurses got him up at 5:30 a.m. and tried to get him into a wheelchair. Being a new patient, they didn't realize Johnny was unable to sit up without becoming dizzy or passing out. He had only sat in a chair a couple of times since Christmas, and that took three physical therapists to move him to a chair and then a lift to return him to his bed. When the two nurses couldn't move him on this particular morning, they brought in a third nurse, then a male nurse. They finally succeeded at getting him into a wheelchair by using a slide board for the transfer.

But that was only the beginning. Johnny's neck was so weak, he couldn't hold his head up. Claudia assisted by holding his head up the whole time he was in the wheelchair. His breakfast tray arrived and was placed in front of him. They told Johnny he needed to eat before dialysis because he wouldn't have anything until he got back and he needed something in his stomach. But it wasn't long after he was sitting up that he became weaker and nauseated. He tried to eat but couldn't. His nausea worsened. He was finally taken out of the wheelchair and placed on a stretcher for his trip to DaVita Dialysis Center.

With Johnny on his way to dialysis, and knowing he would be there for four to five hours and in constant care of the nurses, Claudia felt it might be a good time to go home, check on her mother and the house, and get some fresh clothes. She had not been home since December 22nd except for a few minutes on Christmas Eve when she quickly grabbed some clothes on the way to Vanderbilt.

Gerry was doing well; the house was fine. Claudia laid down on her bed for about forty-five minutes and expected it to feel unbelievably good. But she was restless – there were things on her mind that she needed to do. She got up and started packing her clothes to go back to rehab. That's when she got a call from Johnny. He said they were sending him to the Emergency Department at the Johnson City Medical Center! Then he handed his phone over to a nurse who verified what Johnny had just said. Claudia jumped back into her car and headed for the Med Center. She got there at the same time he did.

On that trip back to the Emergency Department, however, Claudia went a little too quickly - she got her picture taken and a speeding ticket going through a traffic light in Jonesborough.

"Welcome home, Claudia!" A grinning friend told her later. Another friend remarked: "Congratulations on being added to the Jonesborough photo album!" She just chalked it up to her old saying: "Well, if it's going to happen, it's going to happen to me! Some things never change!" But after all she had been through, a speeding ticket was a like a walk in the park. Right now, it was just not important!

Johnny's heart was in atrial fibrillation again; his heart rate had gone into the 130's. Too much fluid had been drawn off from him in dialysis and it caused his heart to be stressed. His skin was wrinkled all over just like he had been sitting too long in a tub of water – only it was from dehydration.

Once more they were back in the familiar surroundings of the Johnson City Medical Center. Johnny was given three liters of fluid and medications to help stabilize his heart. They even considered cardioversion until Claudia told them it had not been successful the last couple of times it was done at Vanderbilt. The idea was discarded.

One of his previous physicians was on duty. "You beat the odds again, Johnny," he said.

How many times can this man "beat the odds?" Claudia wondered...although thankfully. She was awash with guilt for leaving him, for not being at the dialysis facility with him. She promised herself and Johnny that she would never leave him like that again!

His tenure at Quillen lasted less than twenty-four hours. The consensus was that he was not ready for rehab; he was too weak and still too "sick." With Johnny's body traumatized again, preparation was made for admitting him to the hospital. The Johnson City Medical Center would be their home away from home again, at least for a while.

A couple days later, Claudia again ran into their friend, Josh Foster, the nurse anesthetist who had visited them in ICU on that first critical night in December. Knowing that Josh would most likely have good insight into dialysis, working at the Medical Center and having dealt with critically ill patients, she asked him how long people usually stay on dialysis.

He was very honest with his response: "Most people at an older age never come off of it, Claudia, especially if they've gone through a lot of trauma like Johnny has."

It was not encouraging, but she *did* want to know. She wanted to know everything that pertained to her husband. She had a second question ready to fire at Josh but it was suddenly preempted with another thought. She remembered Solomon's advice on medical healing versus spiritual healing and who was really in charge. *Why am I still asking people about statistics? You'd think by now with all we've been through that I would know better. None of that stuff is pertinent if you believe in God and His healing!* Still, she felt that taking care of Johnny and seeing to his needs was her job. It was a privilege God had entrusted to her and she took it seriously. She *wanted* to know statistics – they *were* intriguing. It also reminded her of the awesomeness of God and what He could do, had done, and was still doing.

***

Rehab at Quillen was put on hold. For the next three weeks, Claudia slept in a recliner near Johnny's bed at the Med Center with his monitors directly over her head. When the monitor beeped, she jumped to check his heart rhythm and blood pressure. She made note of every medication that was given to him and wanted to know about every procedure he underwent. She knew the physicians were tired of her questions and suggestions, but she hoped they would understand that, in the long run, it was in his best interest. She told them she was his "continuity of care."

The hospital staff did understand. They didn't have time to read all 800+ pages of his medical records from Vanderbilt. Having been with her husband every moment of his illness and with every physician and with every procedure he had been through, the medical personnel at the Med Center learned that all they had to do was ask Claudia. She knew everything that had been done and the results.

Johnny's dialysis treatments were continued at the Med Center and, just like at Vanderbilt, every time he went to dialysis he came back with a different heart rhythm...every single time! It was starting to look like Josh's tactful but honest answer about Johnny's possible future on dialysis might come true. They were told by doctors that Johnny's kidneys were in the "recovery stage" and there was no way of telling if they would recover or not. They were given neither encouragement nor discouragement. The damage had been done; now it was time to wait and see if his kidneys could recover. Being truthful to themselves, Johnny and Claudia both knew that the chances of ever being taken off dialysis were slim to none.

They stayed steadfastly true to their faith day after day, treatment after treatment...and Johnny started improving! His creatinine slowly started dropping toward normal. Although not wanting to get their hopes up, the nephrologist finally *did say* that if it stayed where it was for a couple of days, they would try weaning him off dialysis! They clung to that hope.

January 25th was a special day! Not only was it exactly one month to the day that Cardio-Thoracic surgeon Dr. Raudat performed the life-saving surgery on Johnny, it was also the first time they saw him again since leaving the Johnson City Medical Center for Vanderbilt. They updated him on all that they had gone through during the month since that time. It was also when they learned Dr. Raudat's story. There had not been much time for conversation on Christmas Day, but now he explained:

"It all worked out. I called Vanderbilt and they had a physician who was available, a room that was available, nurses available, the plane was available, and the weather was right for flying. As for my personal side of the story, I saw a need and knew it was something I could fix. Yes, it *was* Christmas day and my children were home from college and I hadn't seen them in a long time. I called my wife and told her what was happening and, of course, she understood. She said 'Christmas is for giving. Pay it forward and go do your job.' I told her I would be seeing her in about six hours."

It was no surprise when later Claudia and Johnny heard that Dr. Raudat had been nominated for the "Servant's Heart Award" – an award created by Civitan International to recognize unsung people within the community who make a difference by serving others.

Thursday, February 1
It was an exciting day as "hope" started turning into reality. When Johnny was returned to his room after dialysis, Claudia looked at the monitor as she always did and her heart did a different beat of its own! She turned around and looked at the nurse in surprise. "Is that a P wave?" she asked. (A P wave is the first deflection wave associated with right and left atrial depolarization of the heart. It was what had been missing while Johnny was in atrial flutter/fib heart rhythm!)

"I think so," said the nurse, hardly controlling the surprise in his voice. He grabbed his phone and called the telemetry station for confirmation. It WAS a P wave! This was the first time since December that Johnny had a normal heart rhythm! He had been cardioverted four times at Vanderbilt and, up until now, only one cardioversion had been successful but only lasting for a short time. There was finally light at the end of that long, dark tunnel! Never again did he lose his P wave.

It should also be noted that during the time Johnny was having heart arrythmias, several physicians and cardiologists suggested he have an ablation. This procedure is done by going through the groin up to the heart and using electrical current in the atrium to break the circuit causing the abnormal rhythm. But when they realized he had severe groin wounds and was still on the wound vac, they said they could not do it until the wounds were healed. That would take a few months at least. Meanwhile, they would have to try to regulate the condition with medications. This was still touch-and-go with his orthostatic hypotension and it would be nearly impossible to regulate the two together.

By the time Johnny's wounds were healed, his rhythm had converted to normal on its own and the ablation was no longer needed. A couple of months later, a 30-day Event Monitor was done to ascertain if Johnny was staying in a normal rhythm and normal heart rates. There were no problems noted for those thirty days!

"Not having to have the ablation was another blessing and we were so thankful – it was one less procedure that we didn't have to go through. Talk about jumping for joy, we celebrated!" Claudia beamed with delight.

<u>Wednesday, February 7</u>

Johnny beat the odds again! His creatinine remained low enough for him to officially come off dialysis! The nephrologist said it was always a good day when he could take someone off dialysis because it didn't happen often, especially with an older person. He left the room with a smile and closed the door behind him, knowing Claudia and Johnny would definitely be celebrating the good news and deserved some privacy.

Yes, their spirits were definitely high. They looked around their small hospital room, knowing the end was in sight. Small hospital rooms had been their home for quite a while and they had learned to consolidate their living space. They even laughed at the thought of living in one of those trendy tiny houses. After all this time, they knew they could do it if they had to.

Nah! They looked forward to going to their own house one day soon and just stretching out.

Now they felt ready for the next step before going home – back to Quillen for rehab.

The second good news of the day was that Johnny had been cleared for rehab and Quillen was waiting for him once again.

***

<u>Thursday, February 8</u>

Johnny was transferred from the Johnson City Medical Center back to Quillen Rehab. At this point, it was actually easier to move Johnny than it was Claudia. Staying with her husband day and night since December 22nd, she had acquired a lot of "possessions," both hers and Johnny's. She had collected everything she thought they might need during their extensive stay. They had a lot of "stuff" – bottles of shampoo, skin cleaners, urinals, wipes, and all the rest of the hospital collections one accumulates during an extensive stay. And that was just Johnny's stuff! Then there was Claudia's. She collected everything she thought *she* might need since she was not going to leave him. She even had a small pantry set up with things for Johnny to eat in case he could. If he said he wanted it, she got it!

When Discharge arrived and the staff saw what was ready to be moved, they brought in a big person wheelchair for her to carry everything down to the car. She had it packed from side to side and so high that she could hardly see over the top or around the sides to guide it. There were bags hanging off the IV poles on both sides and luggage sitting on the foot rest. She said the looks on people's faces as they rolled through the lobby of the hospital were hilarious. "I must have looked like one of the Beverly Hillbillies," she laughed.

When they got to the lobby, she asked the desk clerk to "watch her cart" while she went to get the car. "He was such a gentleman to accept the challenge," she recalls with a grin.

Everything was going well until she got to her car. The battery was dead...*totally, not even a grunt.* She had that first flutter of fear: *What am I going to do? I can't call Johnny.* Realization set in. *I am on my own.* She pulled herself together. *Come on, Claudia. You can do this. You have done it before. You are not new to this. But it was soooo long ago,* she argued with herself. Indeed, it seemed like a lifetime.

She went to Security and told the security officer on duty her dilemma: "My husband is being transferred to Quillen and I want to be there when he arrives...and my battery is dead...and I'm in a hurry!

The security officer did not seem to share her need to hurry. In fact, Claudia thought with annoyance, *he could not possibly move any slower!* But he did know exactly what to do. He drove over to her car, pulled the hood up, and hooked a set of battery cables to her battery. He had a special device for connecting directly into his truck under the front bumper. She was pretty impressed until she tried to start her car and nothing happened. He removed the cables from his truck and hooked them up again. She tried to start the car. Nothing. *Does this guy really know what he is doing?* She wondered.

Next, he surveyed the rest of the engine compartment. "Well, I think something else is wrong," he finally said.

"What could it be?" Claudia asked, trying to squelch her growing anxiety.

"Well, I don't think it's the battery. I think it's more serious."

Oh great! she thought to herself. *Just what I need!* What she was also thinking was: *Why don't you adjust the cables hooked on the battery. That's what Johnny always does.* But she didn't want him to think she knew more than he did, *"him being a man and me being a woman."* She was not in a position to jeopardize her help. So she kept silent and let him take his time in figuring it out. And he did. Finally, he jiggled the cables hooked to the battery and the car started. What a relief!

She also thought it might be a good idea to strike up a conversation and "build the male ego again." She knew she had sounded abrupt, maybe even pushy. "How long should I let the car run before I can turn it off," she asked.

"Well, how far are you going?"

"Oh, six or seven miles. Just to Quillen Rehab."

"I would ride around for about fifteen minutes before I turned it off."

"Great. That's what I will do. Thank you so much for your help."

She got in the car and started driving hurriedly over to Quillen, knowing Johnny was already there and probably even in his room. She was almost there herself when she realized her Beverly Hillbillies wheelchair with all their personal belongings was still sitting in the lobby at the Med Center. She turned around and headed back to the hospital. *Well, at least I will get my fifteen minutes of driving time to charge the battery,* she admitted with a chuckle! It was another laugh for the day...and time to slow down.

Another car adventure Claudia will always remember while at Quillen occurred on a snowy morning. Four or five inches of snow had fallen overnight and the cars were covered. By habit, she usually tried to park in the same area each time so she wouldn't have to remember where she parked her car. She went out this particular morning and couldn't find her red car. She thought she knew where she parked it, and zeroed in on a red car, but it wouldn't open with the remote. She couldn't see inside because of all the snow and if she cleared the snow away and it wasn't hers, she didn't want anyone to think she was snooping around and looking into car windows.

Great, she thought. *My car has been stolen! It looked like my car but it won't unlock with the remote so it must not be my car.* Normally Claudia is a problem solver and thinks things through, but today her mind just wasn't working. She turned around and headed back into Rehab. When she passed the Administrator in the hall, he asked casually, "Everything okay?" It was not an unusual thing for him to ask. He often checked on patients and caregivers to see how things were going and was genuinely concerned about their progress.

As usual, Claudia said, "Yes, I guess so." She took several more steps, then stopped, turned around, and said, "No, it isn't. I can't find my car."

He accompanied her back out to the parking lot and she pointed out the car she thought was hers. "But it won't unlock," she explained, so it can't be mine. He took her keys and tried to unlock it with the remote, but also without success. Then he proceeded to do what she was afraid to do...remove the snow. She looked in the window. It _was_ her car. He removed the emergency key from the remote and stayed with her until she got in the car and made sure it started. She was embarrassed, but being the kind person he was, the Administrator smoothed it over by reminding her of how much stress she is under and gave her a little hug of assurance. She was still embarrassed.

In addition to getting back to Rehab at Quillen, February 8th was special for another reason – it was Johnny and Claudia's 15th Wedding Anniversary! They had so much to be thankful for on this special day! There was a time just weeks ago when Claudia thought they might never have any more anniversaries or occasions to celebrate. Yes, life was good again and getting better every day.

Being "back home" in Johnson City not only felt good for Claudia and Johnny, it carried the additional benefit of being within visiting distance for friends and family.

Two friends from church came for a visit and brought them flowers, a balloon, and cupcakes to celebrate their anniversary.

The kitchen at Rehab fixed a card and placed it on Johnny's dinner tray: "Happy Anniversary!" The dietary department fixed them both a special dinner that night. Everyone was so nice. They felt almost spoiled while they were there.

Johnny's physical therapy at Quillen was slow-going at best. His blood pressure remained low due to his orthostatic hypotension, which made it a challenge for him to do his PT; he had to sit often. On some mornings, he was not able to participate at all and, one time, he even passed out. He was eventually put on medications that would keep his pressure up enough to keep him from passing out. But little by little, day by day, step by step, he persevered.

Wednesday, February 14

Valentine's Day – was yet another special day and another celebration that would include memories and more thankfulness for supportive family and friends. It started with an email from Claudia's long-time friend, Jane Townsend (aka "Sis"). Jane had been Claudia's ninth grade journalism teacher and writing mentor and, since that time, had become almost like family.

"Sis was on my contact list during Johnny's illness," Claudia explains, "although it was via email rather than text messages. Her email said she had something special planned for us for Valentine's Day. This was so exciting as we had not had any holiday celebrations since Thanksgiving. Although we had no idea what Sis was going to do, it was a time for Johnny and me both to recall our friendship over the years with Sis and her husband, Alan. They are very special people.

"With strategic planning between Sis, who lives in California, and a local restaurant in Johnson City, a Valentine dinner was delivered to us and we celebrated in our Rehab hospital room. We were served fresh roasted red pepper hummus and pita bread, strawberry spinach salad, Salmon and Sea Bass, and cheesecake. It was absolutely divine. What a blessing coming all the way from California. Plus spending another Valentine's Day with my Johnny was a blessing I will never again take for granted.

"Another surprise sent from our California friends was exercise resistance bands used to strengthen the arms and legs. Johnny used them faithfully while at Quillen in rebuilding his strength. Sis had foresight on his need for these. At first, he started with the one of least resistance and could barely stretch it at all. In the middle of the night when he couldn't sleep, and not wanting to wake me, he would get the bands out and exercise on his own. First his arms, then his legs, one side, then the other. He is a man of determination and I am so proud of him."

Johnny did have some exercise opportunities prior to having the exercise resistance bands. Claudia had asked for a trapeze bar for mobility over Johnny's bed at Vanderbilt and one was brought in. At first, he would take his left arm and lift his weaker right arm up to the bar so he could grab it with the right hand. Then he placed his left hand on the bar, eventually gaining the strength to pull himself up in the bed.

To help with his lower body strength, Claudia would lift his legs and do passive motions trying to strengthen them. She purchased a foot bicycle to sit on the end of the bed so Johnny could cycle while lying in the bed when he became strong enough to turn the pedals. The cycle could also be placed on a table top so he was able to work his arms. It wasn't a lot, but it was a start.

A second Valentine's Day special was a visit from the friend and neighbor who was taking care of their dogs after they returned home from the Camp Bowwow Kennel. "She surprised Johnny by bringing his dog, Beau, to Rehab for a visit," Claudia smiled. "It was a decent day and we had Johnny outside for some fresh air, with his chair facing away from the parking lot. He didn't see Beau trotting across the parking lot until he was right next to him. It was a sweet reunion. Beau just laid his head on Johnny's lap with a silent message between the two of them that simply said, 'Pet me. I have missed you.'"

During the first couple of weeks at Rehab, Jan Magee, the friend and hospice nurse who took care of Claudia's dad when he was in the nursing home, and who later texted, "May this be Johnny's Christmas Miracle," came for a visit. She brought Claudia a present – a Wonder Woman™ throw for her hospital bed. Being determined not to leave Johnny again after the last episode of "well, you beat the odds again" and three more weeks in the Johnson City Medical Center, Claudia brought her own queen-sized blow-up mattress and sheets to Quillen and camped in his room. She became a part of the total Johnny/Claudia picture. When they brought water for Johnny, they brought water for Claudia. When Johnny ordered his food, Claudia ordered her food. When Johnny went to exercise, Claudia went to watch him exercise. When Johnny eventually graduated from Rehab and got a T-shirt, they gave Claudia one too. Jan called her Wonder Woman and couldn't resist contributing the very appropriate throw to Claudia's stash of supplies in her camp.

A short time later, Jan herself would be undergoing chemo treatment for breast cancer and Claudia bequeathed the blanket back to Jan. They decided that in the future they were going to pass the blanket around as needed and put each person's name on it in a star. It will say, "We are all Wonder Women!"

Another visit was from the church's Parish Nurse, who brought Johnny a knitted hat. It was knitted by "Busy Hands with a Purpose," a group of ladies in the church who do mission work with their hands. They knit, crochet, loom hats, scarves, baby blankets, and "lapghans" for local groups, including nursing homes and children's groups. They also make isolette covers for the local Neonatal Intensive Care Unit, IV bag covers, and numerous other needed items for the Med Center. Johnny wore the hat while he was in JCMC and Rehab. It helped to keep his head warm. Through all his illness – from medication, stress, and everything else that went on, Johnny's body took a real hit. His hair turned white and started falling out. After he returned home, it started growing back in and some of the dark color came back, even with a little curl.

Johnny's right side remained weaker than his left side from the beginning of his recovery and all the way through rehab. The weakness gradually resolved with exercise and perseverance.

Home at Last

<u>Saturday, March 17</u>

Even though it was St. Patrick's Day, the Christmas tree was still up at the Randolph house. It was Johnny's first Saturday home and time to celebrate the Christmas they didn't have.

Claudia, Johnny, Joshua and Jennifer, and two grandchildren, Emma and JJ, enjoyed their very special day together. Johnny had been telling the kids to go and get their Christmas presents at the house but they decided to wait until Johnny was home and they could all be together again. Claudia encouraged them also. "If you don't get over there and open your presents pretty soon, Emma and JJ, you will have outgrown the clothes we bought for you before Christmas!" Nope, they all wanted to wait!

"We celebrated with everything Johnny requested to eat," said Claudia, "but it wasn't that easy. The trauma to his mouth and tongue from the CMV left him with little or altered taste buds. He thought about Christmas dinner all the time, though. We would sit in the rehab room and make a list of everything he wanted me to cook that day. He listed homemade rolls, turkey and dressing, mashed potatoes, green beans, cranberry sauce, corn, beets, pickles, sweet potato casserole, cherry pie and pumpkin pie, and several more things. I fixed them all. Unfortunately, he was not able to tolerate or even taste most of them. He was having to learn all over what foods he could eat or even liked. He enjoyed eggs. Did I say eggs? *Lots* of eggs, milk, boiled cabbage, cornbread and pinto beans. These have remained the staples for now. He continues to try everything, just to see if he can eat it. He especially likes buffets now because there is a variety for him to sample. He misses sweets and will take little pieces of just about everything on the buffet bar, but they still turn sour in his mouth. Hopefully one day this will be resolved but, in the meantime, another blessing is that it has helped him keep his weight down.

Claudia also notes with a chuckle that because their discharge date from Quillen had been so unpredictable, no one really knew when they were going to be coming home. They stopped at the grocery store en route from Quillen to home and Johnny sat in the car while Claudia went in and picked up a few staples. They went home and had...soup beans and cornbread!

"After Johnny's return home, our Sunday School class continued the food chain that had been set up for Gerry by the dear neighbor, Tami, who helped take care of our dogs after they had been returned home from Camp Bowwow. Now it was for the three of us. They kept meals coming to our home for another month."

The Randolph dogs were brought home about two weeks before Johnny was released from Quillen. Friends took care of them until Johnny was home for good. "The dogs were so excited to have us home again...both of us," Claudia added. "It took a long time for them to settle down. Johnny insisted that I put Beau on a leash and bring him into the house to sit by his chair, but Beau turned out to be too much for him to handle yet. It was a couple of months before he was able to really interact with Beau."

On March 24th, nine days after Johnny came home, there was a 75th birthday celebration in Erwin for his sister, Rosie. It was only twenty minutes away, but Johnny was still weak and tired easily. He was determined to attend, however, and he did. He and Claudia even slow danced. He used Claudia as a prop instead of his walker, and didn't move far from his chair, but that was fine. It felt good!

Johnny "dancing" with Claudia on his sister's birthday

Johnny still had the wound vacs when he arrived home from Rehab. The wound vac dressings and canister that contained the fluids were changed three times a week. Slowly the wounds healed from the inside out. It was a slow process and took until May, but what a great day it was when they were able to pack up the wound vac and mail it back to the company! It had been Johnny's constant companion since a few days before leaving Vanderbilt. No more charging batteries, changing dressings, and carrying the canister around!

"Getting in and out of the house was a challenge, even using a walker," Claudia recalls. "Being orthostatic (blood pressure falling when a person stands up), it was difficult sometimes to even get him to the door, let alone down the steps and into the car. On one occasion, after several tries to get him out of the house for a doctor appointment, I gave up and cancelled the appointment. I called Mike, a trustee at our church who can fix or build anything, and he showed up a couple of days later with another one of the trustees. They built a ramp for us and then I was able to move Johnny in and out of the house quickly in a wheelchair. We continue to appreciate how blessed we are to have such a strong and supportive group of friends."

Arrangements had been made with Home Health to continue therapy at home. Being mindful of Johnny's orthostatic condition, blood pressure readings were taken three times a day, either by Claudia or Home Health, in a lying, sitting, and standing position. Some of the readings had a drop up to between 40-50 mm/Hg. The normal should be less than 20 mm/Hg. This is quite a drop and one time he passed out at home from this. He just got up from his chair, walked about ten feet and hit the floor. "The next thing I knew, I was picking myself up off the floor," Johnny said.

Physical Therapy came three times a week initially. They started with just getting him to stand and, depending on his blood pressure, some days he did exercises just sitting. They concentrated on balance and strengthening exercises with bands and weights. Eventually, he got to a point where PT would walk him through the downstairs part of the house with his walker. Next came climbing steps – just a few at a time. As time went along, his walks became longer and longer.

HOME AT LAST

One of the incentives Johnny had during rehab at Quillen was planning out his garden on paper. It was occupational therapy for his hands and fingers as well as for encouragement and keeping his mind occupied. He planted and replanted everything – beets, corn, tomatoes, beans, and okra. But it was a lot easier on paper and in his mind than in reality. One day, he walked PT out to his future garden spot. He showed them all his plans and where he was going to plant his corn, beans, beets, tomatoes, okra, and squash. While they were impressed, they were also concerned because of the unlevel ground and his balance. But Johnny was determined those things were not going to stop him and they didn't.

When planting time came, Johnny's balance was improving but he was still too weak to safely get out to his garden and back with his walker so Claudia brought their Kawasaki Mule™ up to the house. Now he was able to ride down to the garden and eventually out to his tractor when he got the strength to pull himself up on it.

It was planting time and Johnny decided it was "a go," but when he started to plant the beet seeds, he was not strong enough to walk half the length of the garden on his walker. Claudia became his legs and planting arms. Johnny moved along slowly, told Claudia how he wanted it done, and she did it. Although she helped him do the planting, by harvest time he was strong enough to do it on his own.

Mastering the tractor was another challenge. The day he decided to drive it, Johnny managed to get out to his tractor on his walker. After many tries, he finally succeeded in pulling himself up on it. It was a wonderful feeling of achievement! But when Claudia went out to check on him, he was just sitting on the tractor. "I sure am glad you came out here. I don't have the energy to get off and get back to the house." She helped him down, put him in the Kawasaki Mule, and drove him home.

Eventually, PT gave them exciting news: "You are doing well. There isn't anything else we can help you with – just keep on doing what you're doing." After what seemed like an eternity of working with physical therapy, exercises, and strength building, he was discharged! Claudia believes the garden and working with his tractor was the motivation in his healing process. He continued to go to his shed and work on "something" every day, gradually building his strength.

Being thankful that he was able to be home after their long ordeal and able to get his garden planted, Johnny promised God that if his garden grew, he would share it with people in need. It took determination and perseverance, but it was plentiful and blessed many.

As he got stronger, Johnny saw an opportunity to give back to the church that supported him. A couple of large bushes in front of the church were dying and had to be pulled out and the area cleaned up. A lot of dirt had to be moved. He fired up his tractor and drove it the two blocks to church and moved the dirt from the front of the church to an area in back with his bucket loader. Then he got down and raked mulch until it looked nice.

Johnny and his tractor back at work in Jonesborough

Johnny working in front of his church and appreciating how good it feels to do yard work!

Welcome home, Johnny!

JOHNNY COME BACK

Going Back

Quillen Revisited

At the end of May, they went back to Quillen Rehab where Johnny had been from February 7th until discharge on March 15th. But this time, it was just for a visit. The staff couldn't believe what Johnny looked like compared with the last time they saw him. He was standing up on his own two legs! When he arrived in February, he couldn't stand at all. Vanya, the physical therapist, recalled how she had to hold him up so he could walk along the parallel bars because the muscles in his arms and legs were too weak to support himself. He couldn't even hold his head up, let alone his body. Vanya walked in back of him, holding him with a safety belt around the waist until he was finally strong enough to hold his body up. On the day he returned to Quillen for a visit, it was totally different. Johnny was strong and confident – no walker, only a cane.

Vanderbilt Revisited

Back at Vanderbilt for a checkup, doctors were pleased and amazed with Johnny's progress since they last saw him. Some of the physicians were even discussing writing a Clinical Case Study about Johnny and his medical condition. (A Clinical Case Study is a means of disseminating new knowledge gained from clinical practice. It discusses the signs, symptoms, diagnosis, and treatment of a disease.)

He was also off the expensive, life-saving anti-viral medication he was started on at Vanderbilt. Because of his catastrophic first-day dialysis in Johnson City that landed him back in the hospital, plus his extended rehab time, all his doses of the medication were covered and none had to be purchased. After three negative tests for CMV, the medication was discontinued.

A special treat at Vanderbilt was an opportunity to spend some quality time with his friend, Solomon. Claudia still keeps in touch with Solomon and even named one of her Cavaliers after him...a special tribute indeed! Her puppy Solomon The Peacemaker is fondly known as "Solly."

Johnny and Solomon reunited, this time with Johnny standing!

When Johnny was discharged from Vanderbilt in January, follow-up arrangements were made with his ICU Heart Failure Cardiologist at his clinic in Knoxville, Tennessee. The clinic has also worked closely with him on an ongoing basis concerning his orthostatic hypotension. The medications they prescribed made all the difference in Johnny being able to get out of bed in the morning ...or not. At first, they kept daily records three to four times a day but, after months of not much change and Johnny not being symptomatic, he only takes them twice a day

ECMO Revisited

Johnny and Claudia celebrating the life-saving ECMO, but now only as a memory!

Johnny and Claudia were invited to attend an ECMO Celebration at Vanderbilt on June 9th 2018. It was the first one Vanderbilt had ever put on. What an honor and an exciting event! Johnny's son, Joshua, and his grandson, JJ, went with them.

Arriving at the celebration, they weren't sure exactly where they were supposed to be going so they stopped a physician who seemed to be heading in the same direction.

"Do you know where Langston Hall is located?" they asked.

"Are you going to the ECMO Celebration?" the physician responded.

"Yes!"

"Follow me!"

During their conversation with the physician as they walked along, they found out he was the ECMO specialist on the plane who flew Johnny from the Johnson City Medical Center to Vanderbilt on Christmas Day. It was a chance encounter and a pleasure and honor to meet him and to personally say thank you!

They were handed survivor name badges at the door and walked into a room filled with big balloons shaped in the letters of ECMO, white tablecloths, colorful flowers on the tables, and lots of food. It was a joyous celebration!

Many of the physicians over the ECMO unit spoke, particularly pointing out that it isn't often they get to see the people who have recovered. That was one of the reasons it was decided to have the celebration and everyone attending was invited to come back again next year. "God willing, we will be there," Johnny and Claudia agreed.

The ECMO survivors were encouraged to come to the podium and tell their story.

"Many stories started just like ours," said Claudia – "a brief sentence or two from the survivor, and then 'I can't remember the rest.' The spouse, family member, or friend would finish the story.

"After listening to all the different stories, we felt like Johnny was the lucky (or should we say blessed) survivor. Some had serious issues such as a heart transplants while others started with something more common like the flu. One started with a kidney infection that exacerbated into his having to be on ECMO. But the consensus was: We are all survivors one way or another."

One of the physicians spoke and said, "When I was asked if all this time, energy, effort and expense to try and save one person was really worth it, I thought about my own family – those I hold dear. My answer was: absolutely! In a weird way, even something as cold and clinical as a pump, an oxygenator, or tubes that are in somebody reminds us of what really is important. Love is important! Love matters! And as much as all this stuff costs a lot of money, there is no amount of money that actually matters. There is no amount of money that can buy or even describe loving someone else deeply or eternally. All this 'stuff' called ECMO refocuses our attention on what really is so important – our families, our loved ones."

It was a very special gathering – a very special evening.

The Haven Revisited

While in Nashville, Claudia called her dear friend, Donna, caretaker of The Haven where Claudia stayed – that place of so many memories – good memories during a terrible time. Johnny got to see The Haven for the first time and fell in love with it just as Claudia had. He examined all the pictures on the walls, the verses of hope and inspiration...and even his own picture that Claudia had made while he was in Vanderbilt, delivered on her last day there.

They spent the night at The Haven and Claudia got to sleep in the bed there for the very first time. During her entire stay, she slept on the couch. She didn't feel right being "comfortable" while Johnny was going through such a rough time. She decided she wasn't going to sleep in a real bed until they could sleep in one together. Of course, other than a cot next to Johnny's hospital bed, that was the one at home. How special it was to spend a night in the bed at The Haven with her Johnny!

Claudia, Johnny, and Gerry on a visit to the Opryland Hotel with friend Donna from The Haven

The Wall of Fame at Vanderbilt

Hello Mr. Randolph & Family!

My name is Ashley Troutt and I am a nurse in Vanderbilt's Cardiovascular ICU. We are working on a project entitled Wall of Fame that will feature previous patients and their story of overcoming their challenges in the ICU. We would like to feature the success of these stories on our unit to show other patients/families and staff. Because of your success and the impact you have made on many of the staff, we would like to feature you! If you are interested, please reply to the questions below and submit a photo of yourself with family and/or participating in any of your favorite hobbies. I have also attached a consent form for you to fill out giving us permission to showcase your story on the unit.

Thank you for your consideration in sharing your story with others! Please contact me with any questions you have about the project.

Hope to hear from you soon!

Ashley E. Troutt, RN, BSN, CCRN, Adult ECMO Specialist
Cardiovascular Intensive Care Unit
Vanderbilt University Medical Center

Questions:

1. How has the treatment you received in the CVICU contributed to your overall health today?

Claudia's answer: Because of the care of the physicians and nurses and all involved in Johnny's care, he is here, alive and well. The nurses' encouragement and never-give-up attitude made all the difference for a family member. The physicians were open to any questions and concerns at any time. They listened to me. I am sure at times I was a pest, but I was in the need-to-know phase of my husband's recovery. The more I knew, the more I could process. All the staff was great in keeping me informed and teaching me. Trene was his first nurse and we bonded with her right away. She never left his side and I knew beyond a shadow of a doubt that he was in good hands at Vanderbilt. Dr. Hansen brought Johnny by plane from JCMC to Vanderbilt with only a hope and a prayer.

2. What are some activities/ hobbies you currently enjoy?

Claudia's answer: Johnny is back to his same old routine. Let me see...today he mowed two acres of grass, rototilled our garden which is about 1/4 acre, rode on his Kubota tractor, and took his dog Beau to the creek to swim. Now he is napping, all tuckered out. Johnny is doing all the things he wants to do. There are no deficits from what occurred Christmas day.

3. How have you overcome some of the challenges of your hospitalization and recovery process?

Claudia's answer: Prayer is the only way we have overcome any of this. When something happened, we prayed it up and God answered. <u>All of you were part of God's plan in this.</u> I asked one of the physicians what his chances were. I never really got an answer. Later, Solomon came over and put his arm around me and told me I was asking the wrong physician. He was right and I never did ask again; I never felt that I had to ask that question again. I knew from that point he was going to make it. I stayed with Johnny the entire 84 days of hospitalization. I was his live-in cheerleader. I wouldn't let him give up. He became discouraged in Rehab and he said if I hadn't been there he probably would have just stayed in the bed. It was so hard on him physically since he had lost all his muscle strength.

4. What are three things you could offer as advice to other patients going through a similar experience?

Claudia's answer:
1) Pray, for nothing is impossible. Johnny is proof!
2) Talk with the nurses and physicians. Learn all you can. Be proactive.
3) Don't give up! Don't talk negative around the family member; he/she can hear you!!!! Talk to them and pray over them.

Questions were answered, consent signed, pictures sent, and they are waiting to see what happens with the Wall of Fame.

JOHNNY COME BACK

Notes from Claudia

"I thought Johnny would be different after all of this, but Johnny is still Johnny. He has always been a believer and has had a strong faith. He has always said he had a guardian angel with him. This is not the first time he has been saved from near death. As a child he started to cross the road and a car came by. He said something literally jerked him backwards out of harm's way. There was no one there and no explanation of how it could have happened. I recorded a conversation on February 7 with Pastor Karen Lane from Jonesborough United Methodist Church about that experience and miracles."

Pastor: Miracles are all the things that happen, that are allowed to take place.

Johnny: Yea, that's true. We call them blessings every day. We've got something that is brand new today that's in my favor (referring to officially getting off dialysis).

Pastor: Right.

Johnny: People have said that they want me to testify in church, but I am not much of a public speaker. But I would like, one day, to tell them thank you for all the prayers. If you want any information, you'll have to ask Claudia because I slept through most of it.

Pastor: I understand that (said with a chuckle).

Johnny: I can still remember that monster and that machine. I'm not over that yet. (Quiet chuckles from both the pastor and Claudia. This was when Johnny was on ECMO the very first week in Vanderbilt, and was sedated.) He had a big old square head. Now I realize it was a big old machine making that noise.

I saw stuff crawling on the walls. And I saw a man standing in the corner by the door. He was looking at me and I was thinking it was a doctor or something but he wasn't wearing a white doctor coat. The man was tall, nicely dressed, and never left. I can tell you this much: When they had me under, when they had my blood outside my body, I could hear everything that was going on.

I don't know if I could see much through everything they had over my face or not, but I noticed a light and that light was getting smaller and smaller. Claudia got over me and said: Johnny, don't go. Don't go. Come back to me. Don't go. I could hear her crying over me. She would stand over me and read emails people had sent and read to me from The Bible. Sometimes I think my prayers don't get any higher than this ceiling. There are a lot of people...their prayers go sky high. And I think it was other people's prayers that got me back to where I am.

So, through all this ordeal, I think I always lived my life just care free. I always believed in God, I always believed in Angels, and I always believed in prayer. But I didn't always do it.

I'll tell you a little story, Pastor. When I was a young boy, there was a grocery store up next to where we lived. It wasn't too far from the main road. I came out of that grocery store one day and took off across the road. I got right to the center line, and there was something that grabbed me and jerked me back. I don't know what it was, but that driver called me all kinds of names. To this day I don't know what got hold of me and pulled me back. That's the reason I have always believed in angels. I don't know if it is a regular thing, but that was a physical thing that stopped me from running. It wasn't my time.

For some reason, He kept me around, and I don't know why. I came closer to dying than most, and everybody I have talked to say most people my age don't make it. And yesterday, I walked a little bit, from this chair to there (pointing to the door in the room).

Pastor: That's great; that's progress.

"Then the doctor came in," explained Claudia. "It always seemed that whenever Pastor came to visit, a doctor would show up!"

--- --- --- --- --- --- --- --- ---

"No, Johnny doesn't remember much of what happened through any of this starting in December and still cannot fathom how sick he really was. Maybe that's a good thing. But I remember. I remember all the scary moments, of course – all the times when I was scared, concerned, shaken, but I learned to always turn back to my source of peace. That's all I had to do – spend quiet time with God, knowing He was in charge, not me, not the doctors.

"One of my best memories will always be the day Solomon and I stood together watching Johnny who was still in an induced coma. I asked him what he thought Johnny's testimony would be someday. "He IS the testimony" was Solomon's reply.

"Through this whole ordeal, however, while Johnny was going through his medical ups and downs, his good days and bad days, it was me who was changed. My faith grew. Some of the scripture and words that I received and held in my heart during that time were:

"Prayer doesn't change God; it changes me." ...C. S. Lewis

'Depending on God is not a sign of weakness but one of immeasurable strength and confidence." ...Unknown author

"O Lord my God, I cried to you for help, and you restored my health; you brought me up from the grave." Psalms 30:2-3

"Love never gives up, never loses faith, is always hopeful, and endures through every circumstance." 1Corinthians 13:7

"Ask and it will be given to you; seek, and you will find; knock, and it will be opened to you. For everyone who asks receives, and he who seeks finds and to him who knocks it will be opened." Matthew 7:7-8.

On a humorous note: "Johnny, come back to me – what was I thinking?!" has become a frequent saying in our house. We use it jokingly and at times when we become frustrated with each other. I said that one day when Johnny and I were disagreeing on something: "*Johnny come back to me!*, *What was I thinking*?" To my surprise, his response was: "What was *I* thinking?!" And then he would look right at me and smile and say, "Whatever it was, it must have been right!"

And no matter what he was thinking, it *was* right! I am so glad he decided to come back to me!

"Text and Facebook messages were so important during those eighty-four days and even afterward. Texts were sent and received daily – sometimes hourly from friends and family. Facebook reached out to friends farther away, many of whom were high school and neighborhood friends from Newport News, Virginia, where I grew up. I still get messages asking how Johnny is doing now. Johnny doesn't have a Facebook page but enjoys looking at mine.

"I went through a lot of texting frenzies, and they weren't always during the day. One friend from church said his phone went off in the middle of the night, indicating a text message. He had a feeling it was about Johnny. He didn't pick it up to see who it was from but instead said a prayer and eventually went back to sleep. The next morning, he looked at his phone and, to his relief, it was a message from Verizon. Faith can be as simple as acknowledging that there is a need, saying a prayer, and asking God for that need to be met. It's that simple.

"A very sweet memory concerns a little five-year-old boy named John Luke, son of our good friends Josh and Tamara. Josh is the nurse anesthetist who visited us in ICU. All three of them sent messages to me through Facebook and they all prayed for us, but one morning John Luke handed his mother a devotional book, pointed to one page, and said, 'Read this to me.' He didn't know what it said but he wanted that particular page to be for Johnny and me. It was at a time when our journey had been going on for many weeks and I was exhausted. Amazingly, the devotional he chose was about patience.

"The youth group at our church – the older ones, mailed cards, sent e-cards, and prayed for Johnny every Sunday. They still call him 'The Miracle Man.'"

"One evening – June 14, Johnny had been out on the mower, apparently thinking about everything that had happened to him during those eighty-four days and trying to make sense out of it all. He said a cold chill came over him. Later, while sitting in our living room, he wanted to talk about it so I taped our conversation."

Johnny: It's not the doctors here on earth who took care of me, Claudia. I know that. Like Solomon said, you're talking to the wrong doctor. But it makes me wonder why. How could I have gotten so sick so fast? How could I have gone downhill so fast? They wanted to do an ablation on me but my heart fixed itself. The doctor didn't fix that.

I was out on the mower and I got the chills as I wondered why He brought me back. I was so close to dying and the doctors said I wouldn't make it...unless it had something to do with you and all the people praying for me. There are so many good people out there. It was just like that guardian angel was right there with me again, letting me know there is something more to it than just "hey, he got better."

Have you ever felt the spirit? My version of feeling the spirit is what I had today, and I didn't ask for it. It was just running through my mind. Why me? *I wish I knew what it was because I would hate to miss it.* You never know. It might be just a word spoken to somebody – or mowing someone's yard like Mike did for Raymond. It could be anything. I need to keep my eyes open. If I see a need, I want to take care of it. That is like what Dr Raudat's wife said: Pay if forward. I am at the point now I can do things.

I must have done something good in my life at some point. Well, I know He says He knows everything about you from before you are born until after you die. Your life is planned out for you if you will listen to Him. We all think well, Johnny said a bad word or Johnny did this or Johnny did that. That doesn't mean anything. We all do that. One sin is the same as another. Everybody sins. Just realize it and don't make a habit of it. I've heard people say I wouldn't go down there to that old church with that bunch of sinners. Well, they have to be sinners or they wouldn't be going to church. I have always believed in the Lord and have always believed in angels. I am not going to sit here and say I have always done what is right because I have been a sinner all my life. But I have always believed. I always thought that it had to hit your heart, that you would have this great feeling and all this stuff. But as I have gotten older, I realize you don't always have that. You get your feeling from God, I think from the good deeds you do. I mean, if you do something good for somebody, you do feel good. If you do something bad to somebody, it makes you feel bad. Just do the best you know how.

I think we both learned something from this. I try not to take so much for granted now because I do realize just how fast you can be here today and gone tomorrow. There are a lot of people who don't get that second chance. This is like it isn't even real to me yet. I think I fared better in there than you did. I didn't have the stress or the worry. I didn't worry about anything, even when I was in my right mind. That's crazy isn't it?

Claudia: I don't guess you had to, I worried enough.

Johnny: That's what I am saying. You and the young'uns worried yourself to death.

Claudia: I don't know if I worried actually; maybe that is not the right word.

Johnny: You did worry that I might have passed on?

Claudia: Well, it was a possibility, but I didn't actually worry about it. I didn't have time to.

Johnny: Wasn't scared?

Claudia: No, never was, *never was.*

Johnny: Really?

Claudia: *Never* was.

Johnny: You just didn't care?

Claudia: It's not that I didn't care; I just wasn't scared. I don't get scared. I may be concerned about something, but I don't get scared. Working in the ER, people would come in with all kinds of injuries and problems; some were life-threatening, but they never scared me. So your condition didn't scare me, but I was very aware of the seriousness of your condition and even the possible outcome.

Johnny: Really? According to what the doctors told you, technically I shouldn't have made it.

Claudia: I know, but I knew that you would. It was just a process we had to go through to get you better every single day until I could get you home.

Johnny: Did you ever think that I was not going to get better when you saw that I couldn't even move myself?

Claudia: No.

Johnny: You never had that thought?

Claudia: No. Being a nurse, I know that state. I know it is something you have to work at and start all over again. It was not new to me.

Johnny: You know, I could have been less determined, and I would still be in that hospital. There are some people who go to physical therapy who don't do anything, but I told them that I came to work. You remember that first day Vanya tried to get me up?

Claudia: Yeah, you were too weak to stand up by yourself or even hold your head up. You had to lay your head on her shoulder and hug her so you wouldn't fall down.

Johnny: I will tell you the truth, it took every bit of strength I had. It did.

"Johnny kind of got quiet after that," said Claudia, "reminiscing about all the things that had happened and still thinking about 'Why?' Why me? I remembered the words he said earlier: "I hope I don't miss it," referring to an opportunity to do something good for someone in need. I hope I don't miss it either."

"I have two last prayer requests for God. The first is for Johnny's orthostatic hypotension that remains with him daily. He is not presently always symptomatic, but only because of the medications keeping his blood pressure higher. The physicians are hoping at some point his body will recover from the orthostasis and he can be weaned off the medication. When that happens, they can start Johnny on a new medication that will help support his heart. That new medication also lowers blood pressure so it can't be started without first solving the problem of the hypotension.

"His myasthenia gravis is also there every day and always will be. It causes him weakness, some days more than others, and just a generalized whole body 'feel bad' as Johnny describes it. But it is being treated with medication.

"My second prayer is regarding the myocarditis that attacked his heart. We know that it may return. That is what we have been told. It's not a large chance, but a chance nonetheless. It's something that cannot be prevented from happening with medication so all we can do is wait and see if it does happen. Please pray with us that it does not recur. *Our God is an awesome God and He does answer our prayers.*"

"Johnny and I believe in miracles. We have lived them. There is no way all the miracles we experienced could be 'chance' or 'coincidence.' We are living proof that nothing short of divine interventions have occurred throughout our eighty-four-day journey and brought us safely to where we are today. We are thankful for <u>all</u> of God's blessings, especially the one that has returned Johnny to a quality of life that is much like where this all began."

Faith! It's a personal experience. You can't see it or touch it. You can only attain it by believing within yourself. We have witnessed what faith and prayer can do, and it is real. God is for Real!

Claudia and Johnny Randolph

JOHNNY COME BACK

Glossary of Medical Terms

Atrial fibrillation – occurs when the atria beat out of rhythm with the ventricles. Atrial flutter results from an abnormal circuit inside the right atrium, or upper chamber of your heart.

Atrial flutter - results from an abnormal circuit inside the right atrium, or upper chamber of your heart. It beats extra-fast, about 250-400 beats per minute. A normal heartbeat is 60-100 beats per minute.

C-pap – Continuous positive airway pressure. CPAP is an effective treatment for moderate to severe obstructive sleep apnea.

Cardiogenic shock – a condition in which the heart suddenly can't pump enough blood to meet the body's needs. It is rare and often fatal if not treated immediately.

Cardiologist – a person specializing in heart action and diseases.

Cardioversion – a medical procedure by which an abnormally fast heart rate or other cardiac arrhythmia is converted to a normal rhythm using electricity or drugs.

Congestive heart failure – A chronic condition in which the heart doesn't pump blood as well as it should.

CT scan – uses computer-processed combinations of many x-ray measurements taken from different angles to produce cross-sectional images of specific areas of a scanned object, allowing the user to see inside the object without cutting.

Cytomegalovirus (CMV) – a common virus that can infect almost anyone. Once infected, the body retains the virus for life. It is easily transmitted to others through close physical contact or by contact with infected objects if the person's immune system is significantly weakened. If this happens, the virus can reactivate.

ECHO – echocardiogram – a procedure that checks ejection of blood from the heart. Normal values are 55-60%.

ECMO Machine – extracorporeal membrane oxygenation – a temporary mechanical support system used to aid heart and lung function on patients with severe respiratory and/or cardiac failure.

Extubation – weaning a person off of a ventilator

Fasciotomy – a surgical procedure where the fascia is cut to relieve tension or pressure commonly to treat the resulting loss of circulation to an area of tissue or muscle. A limb saving procedure when used to treat acute compartment syndrome – a condition resulting from increased pressure within a confined body space, especially of the leg or forearm.

Gastrointestinal – an organ system which takes in food, digests it to extract and absorb energy and nutrients, and expels remaining waste as feces. The mouth, esophagus, stomach and intestines are part of the gastrointestinal tract.

Hypotensive – Abnormally low blood pressure

ICU – Intensive Care Unit

Impella – a device inserted through the groin into an artery and threaded up to the heart to temporarily assist in moving blood through the heart and the rest of the organs in the body.

Intensivist – a board-certified physician who provides special care for critically ill patients. The intensivist has advanced training and experience in the treating this complex type of patient.

Intubated – a procedure whereby a tube is placed down the trachea (windpipe) and to maintain an open airway to facilitate ventilation to the lungs including mechanical ventilation.

Lewy Body – a disease associated with abnormal deposits of a protein in the brain. These deposits lead to problems with thinking, movement, behavior, and mood and the person is known to have hallucinations and delusions.

Mean arterial pressure (MAP) – the average blood pressure in an individual during a single cardiac cycle.

Myasthenia Gravis – an autoimmune disease producing weakness and rapid fatigue of muscles under voluntary control.

Myocarditis – inflammation of the heart muscle that attacks the muscles and weakens the immune system.

Orthostatic Hypotension – a systolic blood pressure (top number) decrease of at least 20 mm Hg or a diastolic blood pressure (bottom number) decrease of at least 10 mm Hg within 3 minutes of standing.

Respiratory – having to do with the lungs and breathing.

Sepsis – A toxic condition resulting from the spread of bacteria.

Septic shock - a widespread infection that can cause organ failure and dangerously low blood pressure.

Swanz catheter – A Swan-Ganz catheterization is the passing of a thin tube or catheter into the right side of the heart and the arteries leading to the lungs. It is done to monitor the heart's function and blood flow and pressures in and around the heart.

Thoracic – Having to do with the part of the body between the neck and the abdomen or the cavity in which the heart and lungs lie.

Titers – The concentration of a solution as determined by a titration.

Tracheostomy – an opening into the trachea through the neck to allow the passage of air.

Tracheotomy – a surgical procedure of cutting into the trachea through the skin.

Troponin – a marker indicating a heart attack – done with a blood draw.

Ulcer – an open sore on an external or internal surface of the body, caused by a break in the skin or mucous membrane that failed to heal.

Vascular – having to do with blood vessels.

Made in the USA
Columbia, SC
14 December 2018